Anonymous

Report of the Michigan Andersonville Monument Commission

On Erection of Monument at Andersonville

Anonymous

Report of the Michigan Andersonville Monument Commission
On Erection of Monument at Andersonville

ISBN/EAN: 9783337146504

Printed in Europe, USA, Canada, Australia, Japan

Cover: Foto ©ninafisch / pixelio.de

More available books at **www.hansebooks.com**

REPORT

Michigan Andersonville
Monument Commission

ON ERECTION OF

MONUMENT

AT ANDERSONVILLE, GA.

LANSING
ROBERT SMITH PRINTING CO.
1905

PREFATORY.

As soon as the Woman's Relief Corps had purchased the Prison Pen at Andersonville, known as the Camp Sumpter by the Confederates, an effort was made by the great organization to interest the Grand Army of the several States in an endeavor to induce their authorities to erect monuments to their dead on that historic spot. The idea at once met universal approval. In Michigan an active interest was taken, especially by a number who had suffered imprisonment there. Among these, Dr. J. A. Griffen, of St. Charles, gave his whole heart to the work. Comrade Griffen had been confined there and had visited the stockade since its purchase by the W. R. C. and it was chiefly through his instrumentality that a committee was appointed at the State Encampment at Pontiac in 1902, to go before the Legislature and ask for an appropriation for that purpose. The committee named was E. S. Jameson, George W. Stone and J. A. Griffen. This committee sent out blank petitions to every Post in the State asking the G. A. R. to solicit signatures and to then forward them to their several Senators and representatives. The effect being that the Legislature was deluged with these petitions with the result that the bill calling for an appropriation of $6,000, of which amount not more than $500 should be allowed for expenses of the commission, was unanimously passed by both houses and signed by the Governor. The naming of the commission was vested in Governor Bliss. The W. R. C. having done so much in buying and caring for the grounds, it was fitting that they should have representation on the commission. The Governor therefore very justly and wisely named a very prominent and active worker in that organization as one of the commission:—Mrs.

Jennie Carpenter, of Saginaw, was the lady selected. As the commission was to consist of but three members, the Governor was forced to drop one of those who had served on the Grand Army committee. As Dr. Griffen was from the same county as Mrs. Carpenter, the Governor very reluctantly was obliged to leave his name out.

GOVERNOR LEISS,
MEMBER OF AN ... MONUMENT COMMISSION.

REPORT OF COMMITTEE.

To the Honorable A. T. Bliss, Governor of Michigan:

Dear Sir and Comrade—The Michigan Andersonville Monument Commission, appointed by your Excellency to carry out the provisions of House Enrolled Act Number 184, Session of 1902 and 1903, beg leave to make the following report:

The bill, as unanimously passed by both houses, and signed by you, provided for the appointment of a commission of three residents of Michigan who were to select a site in the former Military Prison at Andersonville, Ga., and there to erect a suitable monument at a cost of not more than $6,000, in memory of the seven hundred Michigan soldiers and sailors who died at that place.

The actual expenses of the commission to be allowed in amount not to exceed $500.

No provision having been made in the bill to give it immediate effect, in order to expedite matters, a preliminary meeting of the commission was held in the Executive Parlor at Lansing on August 6th, 1903. The members of that body as appointed by you, were Mrs. Jennie Carpenter of Saginaw, George W. Stone of Lansing, and E. S. Jameson of Marine City, all were present at the meeting except Mrs. Carpenter.

As the act creating the commission and making the appropriation would not take effect until September 21st, it was decided that no legal action binding the State could be taken until after that date, but this would not prevent the Commission from advertising for plans and specifications from builders for a monument: said plans to be in the hands of Secretary George W. Stone not later than September 21st at Lansing. This action was therefore taken and designs were solicited; bids to cover entire cost of monument, concrete foundation, transportation to, and erection on ground to be selected by the commission, all to be complete and ready to unveil by May 1st, 1904. Entire cost not to exceed $5,500. Committee reserved the right to reject any and all bids. Those submitting plans not accepted to receive no compensation.

Monument to be made of the best white granite, free from black knot, sap flaws or imperfections of any kind. The following firms were asked to submit designs: Lloyd Brothers, Toledo, Ohio; E. R. Fletcher, Harwick, Vt.; The Hughes G. and M. Company, Clyde, Ohio; Millar & Clark, Americus, Ga.; Hobson, E. Saginaw, Mich.; Lansing Granite Company, Lansing, Mich.; Sigbald Asbjornsen, Chicago, Ill.; American Bronze Foundry, Chicago, Ill.; W. R. Martin Granite Company, Philadelphia, Pa.

No further business being possible the meeting adjourned subject to call of Governor A. T. Bliss.

Pursuant to call, the first regular meeting of the commission was held in Executive Parlors, Lansing, September 22nd, 1903, all members of the commission present. On motion of Governor Bliss the commission proceeded to organize and elect officers. The following officers were elected:

Edward S. Jameson, President; George W. Stone, Secretary; Mrs. Jennie Carpenter, Treasurer.

The following named submitted plans, etc., for the monument:

Lloyd Brothers Company, Millar & Clark, and S. Asbjornsen.

After a careful inspection of the designs submitted, a ballot was taken, resulted in three out of the four votes being cast for Design Number 1, of Lloyd Brothers Company. On motion of Governor Bliss the vote was made unanimous and the following contract was entered into by the commission and Lloyd Brothers Company of Toledo, Ohio.

CONTRACT.

Made and entered into this 24th day of September, A. D. 1903, by and between the Michigan Andersonville Monument Commission, as the party of the first part, and the Lloyd Brothers Company of Toledo, Ohio, a corporation organized and doing business under the laws of the state of Ohio, as party of the second part.

WITNESSETH, That the said second party does hereby covenant and agree to build and erect complete for said first party upon ground to be selected by them in the Prison Pen at Andersonville, Georgia, a monument according to the specifications attached hereto and which are to be considered as a part of this contract.

It is also agreed that all of said work shall be completed by May 1st, 1904, unless prevented by labor troubles, fire or other causes beyond the control of said second party, and if so prevented then as soon thereafter as is consistent with a strictly first class piece of work.

In consideration whereof it is hereby agreed that upon receiving notice from the said second party of the completion of the work, that the said first party will within thirty days thereafter inspect the work, and if found to be completed in a first class manner according to this contract and specifications, that they, the said first party, will thereupon accept the monument and pay to the said second party the sum of five thousand and five hundred dollars ($5,500).

In witness whereof the above described parties have hereunto set their hands and seals the day and year first above written.

THE MICHIGAN ANDERSONVILLE
MONUMENT COMMISSION.
By EDWARD S. JAMESON, President.
GEORGE W. STONE, Secretary.
THE LLOYD BROTHERS CO.
By J. H. LLOYD, Secretary.

SPECIFICATIONS FOR MONUMENT TO BE ERECTED BY THE STATE OF MICHIGAN, AT ANDERSONVILLE, GEORGIA.

The design for this work is to be that submitted by the Lloyd Bros. Co., of Toledo, Ohio, and known as No. 1.

The foundation for the work shall be constructed as follows: All the earth within the space covered by the lower base of the monument at the top and six inches larger than that at the bottom of the excavation, shall be removed to a depth of five feet below the surface of the ground, and taken from the premises, and the space so excavated shall then be entirely filled in with masonry or concrete composed of a good quality of native stone suitable for the purpose, and mortar of the first quality of hydraulic cement, and sand of the proper proportion and which shall be properly and thoroughly mixed before being placed in the excavation, the purpose being that when completed the foundation shall be the same size at the top as the base of the monument and six inches larger than that at the bottom. All stones are to be well bedded and all interstices completely filled in or grouted with the cement mortar so that when the same is set, it shall become one solid mass of rock. This foundation shall be put in a sufficient time ahead of the erection of

L. ADAMS

the monument, and the top surface left level and smooth to receive the granite work.

The material above the surface of the ground shall be absolutely No. 1 light Vermont granite, all to be uniform in texture and color, free from any and all knots, streaks or sap, and without any mineral or other impurities that would render it other than strictly first class stone for this purpose.

The size of the monument shall be as follows.

Lower base (in two pieces) 14' .0" x 9' .8" x 1' .4".

Second base (in one piece) 11' .4" x 7' .0" x 1' .0".

Third base (in one piece) 10' .0" x 5' .10" x 2' .2".

Die (in one piece) 8' .0" x 3' .2" x 4' .0".

Workmanship. The four faces of the lower base shall be natural rock face with margin lines around the corners. All the balance of the exposed surfaces shall be the very best bush hammered work known as twelve cut, and shall be straight and true in every respect. The statute shall be artistically carved by sculptors skilled in that class of work from plaster model, and when set in place to be well secured to monument and the joint between them to be entirely closed with cement. The wreath of laurel shown in design shall be standard U. S. Bronze. All stone shall be set upon that below it, resting upon sheet lead, and after all stones are in place the joint shall be closed up by having wedge lead driven into the joint securely caulked to prevent the entrance of moisture and nicely trimmed off.

Inscriptions. The following inscription shall be cut upon the front face of die:

IN MEMORIAM.

Erected by the State of Michigan to her soldiers and sailors who were imprisoned on these grounds.

On the two buttresses on the front of the third base the

dates 1861-1865 shall be cut as shown on plan. Should other
inscriptions be desired the said first party shall furnish them
and notify the said second party in writing within thirty days
from this date. Finally. It is the intention and understanding that this
work when completed shall be of the highest possible class of
monumental art, and perfect in all its details. Both material
and workmanship in all respects shall be of the best grade that
the market affords and when finished the work is to be cleaned
down and all litter and rubbish caused by the erection of the
work shall be removed from the premises.

On October 22nd the commission met in Executive Parlors
at Lansing, members all present except Governor Bliss. It
was then decided that President E. S. Jameson visit Andersonville and inspect the site tendered the State by the W. R. C.
and enter into arrangements for the dedicatory services. On
Nov. 4th, Mr. Jameson accompanied by J. H. Lloyd of Lloyd
Brothers Co., made the trip and found the location everything
that could be desired.

On March 23rd, 1904, the commission again met in the Executive Parlors at Lansing. All members present. General
passenger agents of several roads attended the meeting to present the advantages of their several routes to Andersonville.
It was decided that Secretary George W. Stone assisted by Col.
Avery have full charge of arrangements with the railroad companies, also Pullman cars. It was also decided that our special
train leave Detroit on Saturday, May 28th, going and return-
ing over the M. C., C. H. & D., L. & N., N. C. & St. L., W. A.,
and Central of Georgia, via Macon.

President E. S. Jameson was appointed to take charge of
advertising, printing arrangement of program and circulating
of same. The dedication to occur on Memorial Day, May 30th,
1904, that the schedule of time be limited to six days, and that
Mrs. A. T. Bliss have the honor of unveiling the monument.

The Legislature of Michigan provided for the dedication of the monument by enactment in substance as follows:

The Governor and his military staff, the President of the Senate, the Speaker of the House of Representatives, and a committee of three from the Senate and six from the House, to be appointed by the President of the Senate and Speaker of the House respectively, are hereby directed to represent the people of the State of Michigan, and they are authorized to accept in the name of the State, the monument to be erected at Andersonville, Georgia, in memory of the seven hundred Michigan Union Soldiers who died there, when the same shall be completed by the commission provided for by House Enrolled Act Number 184, and to participate in the dedicatory exercises of said monument.

The train with two special Pullmans attached, left Detroit at 12 m. Saturday, May 28th, the following ladies and gentlemen accompanying the party:

SENATORS.

C. B. Fuller and wife, Charles Smith, F. F. Sovereign, E. C. Cannon and wife, S. Van Aikin.

MEMBERS CF HOUSE.

F. D. Newberry, Wm. N. Siggins and son, H. H. Herkimer, wife, daughter and niece, C. A. Hollinbeck and wife, C. H. Brown, Governor A. T. Bliss, Mrs. A. T. Bliss. Mrs. Peet, General James H. Kidd, General Geo. H. Brown, Col's. S. H. Avery, J. L. Boer, J. N. Monroe, Geo. H. Turner, A. L. Holmes, Wm. A. Wait, Majors H. E. Johnson, C. A. Vernou, Commander F. D. Standish, Frederick Kidd, T. J. Paisley, Dorr Blakeman, C. S. Fuller, A. C. Miller and wife, Baird Hill and wife, Ben. Johnston, J. H. Lloyd, Albert Dunham and niece, Mrs. C. M. Smith and two daughters, H. J. Sugru and wife, Herman Holmes, E. S. Jameson, Mrs. Jennie Carpenter, Geo. W. Stone.

A pleasant run brought the party to Nashville about 8 a. m. Sunday, where the Governor of Tennessee, his staff and the Merchants and Manufacturers' Association met us and, after breakfast, in special trolley cars, showed us the principal points of interest in the city, then to Fiske University, where a special concert program was given by the students, as only those colored people can render those jubilee songs and choruses. Back to the Depot Hotel where a lunch was given us by the distinguished citizens of Nashville and unique souvenirs provided for all. After some most happy remarks from the Governor of Tennessee, which were responded to by Governor Bliss, the party boarded the train for Andersonville, passing through historic ground the entire distance.

Arriving at our destination we found special trains were bringing in a large number of colored people, estimated at six thousand. Two companies of U. S. Regulars had been detailed from the Fort and also a Company of Militia from Macon were present to preserve order. The G. A. R. Posts from Fitzgerald, also the W. R. C. were there in force and every one of the 13,000 graves in the National Cemetery had on it the flag, for which they had nobly died and no grave but what had flowers placed on it. It was a grand and imposing sight. After the Memorial Exercises in the Cemetery, all adjourned to the old Stockade where our beautiful monument had been erected and was now veiled with a large flag. A very heavy shower of nearly two hours duration interrupted the ceremonies, but at its conclusion the following program was rendered.

Opening Prayer, Rev. Frank E. Jenkins.

Vocal Quartette, Miss Mary Lane Evans, Mrs. Mamie Folsom Wynne, George A. Kellogg, and Alfred A. Morrell, of Central Congregational Church of Atlanta.

GEO. W. KING.

Unveiling of Monument, Mrs. A. T. Bliss.

Presentation of Monument to State, E. S. Jameson, President of Commission.

Acceptance of Monument. Hon. A. T. Bliss, Governor of Michigan.

Oration, General James H. Kidd, Orator of the Day.

Singing of America, by all.

Benediction, Rev. F. E. Jenkins.

PRESENTATION SPEECH OF E. S. JAMESON.

Ladies and Gentlemen: Since history was first written, it has been customary among civilized people to perpetuate in indestructible stone or metal the features of those whose heroic acts or great genius have raised them above their fellows. What more fitting tribute to them when they have passed away, than the granite shaft, the bronze statue. In after ages when they shall have become antiques, when the moss of ages shall have mellowed the harshness of the freshly quarried granite, when the green oxydation of time shall have tinted the bronze, the form still stands to remind the after generation of the great deeds of their ancestors and to become an incentive to youth to so strive and act that they may merit from posterity the same reward. History is filled with acts of heroism and gallant deeds performed in battle where men in strife risked and laid down their lives for their country. Many again have sacrificed their lives for their religion. Thousands have heroically perished in the attempts to save the lives of others, but history records nothing more sublime than the martyrdom of the thousands who perished on this spot, who suffered the most exquisite tortures of slow starvation, who slowly but not less surely rotted to death with disease, exposed without clothing or shelter to the scorching suns of summer, the pouring rains and frosts of winter, their comrades perishing beside them by scores every

day, devoured by vermin, parched by thirst, suffocated by the
foulest effluvias and all this borne for principle, where by a
word of renunciation the gates would have been opened and
they could have gone forth to life and liberty. History, I say,
records nothing more grand and sublime. When we gaze
around us today, on this beautiful spot where nature in her
most glorious moods revels beneath the beautiful blue canopy
of Heaven, surrounded by the exquisite verdure of this glorious climate, with the fragrance of the flowers, the music of the
birds entrancing our senses, how hard to lift the veil of forty
years and picture the horrors and gloom that then pervaded
this historic spot. But time most mercifully heals all wounds
and we assemble here with no bitterness rankling in our hearts.
"With charity toward all and malice toward none," still we
cannot overlook the sufferings of those heroes whose gallantry
we are assembled here to perpetuate in imperishable granite.

I wish here to pay a tribute of respect and gratitude to that
noble woman, Lizabeth A. Turner, (who I deeply regret is
unable to be with us today) for the grand work done by her,
and that great organization, the W. R. C., in purchasing and
preserving to posterity these grounds which shall be forever
hallowed in the hearts of the American people. I wish also
on behalf of this Commission to extend to your Excellency, our
thanks for the high honor conferred upon us in our appointment to membership on this board, also for your universal
courtesy and assistance in our work, which I know has been to
the others, as to myself, a labor of love. And now what more
meet and fitting, that on this day, the soldiers solemn Sabbath,
when over the length and breadth of our land our people are
gathered in every cemetery to drop a flower on the grave of
those who perished that our Nation might live, what more appropriate, that we have assembled here to erect and dedicate to
these heroes, an imperishable monument commemorative of
their sufferings and patriotism.

I think it is with pardonable pride that I can state that it is less than two years since the G. A. R. of Michigan appointed a committee to solicite from our Legislature an appropriation for a monument on this spot. The committee was successful, an appropriation was obtained and the result is now before you in this beautiful and classical stone.

And now in fulfillment of my duty as President of this commission, it is with the greatest pleasure that I turn over to your Excellency as the Executive and Representative of the great common wealth of Michigan this monument which has been formally accepted by this commission also the deed of the ground upon which it stands.

SPEECH OF ACCEPTANCE, GOV. A. T. BLISS.

Address by Gov. A. T. Bliss, at Dedication of Michigan Monument, Andersonville, Ga., May 30th, 1904.

Mr. Chairman, Members of the Andersonville Prison Monument Commission, Ladies and Gentlemen:

This is sacred ground, consecrated by the suffering of men who here gave "the last full measure of devotion."

Theirs was not the glory of death on the firing line; the reaper touched them not amid the roar and the shock of battle. Penned in by the dead line, wasted by disease, far from home and loved ones, they were mercifully mustered out, leaving as a heritage to the nation the memory of a devotion as limitless as eternity itself.

Kneeling beside these silent mounds, we may learn anew a lesson of patriotism, and take fresh heart for the duties and responsibilities that confront us. Brave men were those prisoners of war, and patriots to the last drop of blood throbbing in their hearts. It was good blood too, the blood of a race true to its ideals, and these men whom fate had destined to an awesome

death, met their end so devotedly, that the grimness of it, the
terror of it, had power only to place their *mortal bodies in
mother earth. Their souls go marching on.*

Nearly seven hundred men from the peninsular State are
entombed within the precincts of the war-time prison, and *we
of Michigan* are here, *this Memorial Day,* to dedicate to their
memory a granite monument, testifying for all time that a great
people do not forget their heroes, and to proclaim the pride
we take in the faithfulness of those dead sons of our commonwealth.

Nearly forty years have passed since the passions of civil war
ran hot in the veins of the north and the south. Out of the
ashes of that gigantic strife has arisen a re-created nation,
whose foundations have been cemented in the blood of a new
generation shed on the battle fields of Cuba. The mutual sacrifices of a reunited people have added another and a greater
glory to the *stars of a common flag.* Gray headed men, once
foes, have mingled in bonds of fraternity again and again, and
the years have made it possible for the representatives of our
far northern State to come here in the hospitality of this *far
southern State* and dedicate a memorial to patriotic devotion,
that *neither* may forget.

The war and its suffering, the anguish of crucified hearts,
and the burdens of those days belong to the dead past, but the
lessons, the *memories,* and the *patriotism* are a living part of
the national life. A monument to the soldier of either army is
a monument to the *American soldier,* and true men and women
everywhere proudly acclaim it in that *wider, larger,* charity,
that far reaching love of country which constitutes a great nation. We feel that this monument in its greater significance
will to the end of time teach the nation, *our nation* that *we are*
one people, and that the sacrifice of those Michigan soldiers are
for the common glory as they were for the common welfare.

It seems as but yesterday that the stockade reared its head

MRS. JENNIE CARPENTER,
GREASED ANDERSONVILLE MONUMENT

about these grounds and the dead line warned *"thus far and no farther."* I can see the dense masses of the prisoners, and entering into their daily life, know, as only experience can know, the life of a prisoner of war. It is one thing to serve, as a soldier in the field, to endure the privations of camp and march, to face the madness of battle, and endure its carnage; it is another thing to be herded behind walls whose never-sleeping eyes are loaded muskets, to exist beneath skies that are pitiless, dropping alternately scorching heat and the chill of rain, and to suffer day by day, to see death strike right and left, and to realize that one is helpless to do aught but endure it all as best one can, while outside the walls marches are made, battles are fought, and deeds are done for home and flag. The wonder is that men can withstand so much and live. And yet God watched over Andersonville, for if he had not, in the fullness of time, the miraculous spring would not have given of its waters.

In behalf of two and a half millions of people, who are the State of Michigan, I accept this monument and most solemnly declare it dedicated to the memory of the dauntless sons of the commonwealth whose dust forever hallow this ground.

With Lincoln I say: "The brave men, living and dead, who struggled here, have consecrated it far above our poor power to add or detract. The world will little note, nor long remember what we say here, but it can never forget what they did here."

To the members of the commission, whom I had the honor to appoint to carry out this work, I wish to extend my heartfelt thanks for the conscientious manner in which they have performed their work, bringing credit not only to themselves but to the great State of Michigan. When I look at this grand and beautiful monument which for all time will commemorate the miseries of our gallant comrades who suffered here, I feel that too much praise cannot be bestowed on the Commission

2

whose artistic judgement made so judicious a selection, that as
other monuments are raised on this spot by our sister States,
we may never fear that Michigan will suffer by comparison. I
wish also to express my thanks to the Commission for the universal courtesy and the good fellowship extended to me in our
very harmonious intercourse. It will always be a bright spot
amid the cares and labors of executive office and the association ever remembered as a most pleasant one.

ORATION, GEN'L JAMES H. KIDD.

We have come from our homes between the great lakes of
the north upon this pilgrimage to the sunny south. We are
here to dedicate and unveil this monument. The people of the
State of Michigan provided through their representatives in the
Legislature for its erection. It is sacred to the memory of
those sons of hers, who during the closing years of the great
Civil War, died in the confederate prison at Andersonville, and
were buried here beneath a southern sod. They passed from
this life to that other, in the realm of the unseen, amid scenes of
unexampled pathos. A truthful recital of their patient sufferings, unmitigated by a single ray of hope or sunshine, might
well wring tears from the eyes of any mute statue, that might
be set up to typify the manhood that was here put to the proof.
No friendly hand ministered to them in their last moments. No
tender ministrations assuaged their pain. There was no ano-
dyne in the cup of bitterness which they drank. Gaunt misery
and despair waited upon them in their journey into the unknown land. Their only solace was consciousness of duty well
performed; their sole reward the grateful remembrance in
which they are held by their countrymen,—the kind of reward
which comes to men, only after death.

Today, throughout the northern states is Memorial Day—

the day by common consent and usage set apart for these many years, for the living to pay the tribute of their respect to the memory of the dead. Today the people over all the broad land have met to decorate with flowers the graves where rest our soldiers; to hold a memorial service; to salute the flag; to renew their patriotism. Wherever the sun shines and the green grass grows; wherever the violet and the daisy bloom; wherever a feathered songster trills his song of passion or of praise; wherever a church spire points to heaven; wherever there is a heart that can be touched with pathos or moved by a noble example; there this day is reverently observed. From the hamlet and the city; from the homes of the lowly and the rich; from all classes and conditions; from every sect and every party; with one common impulse they have come together and united their voices in a solmn requiem and in a song of praise, —a chant for those who made the supreme sacrifice of their lives; an anthem of rejoicing that by their sacrifices the union was saved. And in this anthem, today, the voices of federals and confederates alike join, while in distributing flowers, either north or south, no distinction is made between those who wore the blue and those who wore the gray. They were Americans all, moved by the right, as God gave them to see the right, and it is to this common American manhood that we pay these tributes.

It is, then, in the language of Lincoln's Gettysburg address, "altogether fitting and proper," that we should be here. Of the 12,000 brave boys in blue, who rest in these sacred grounds, victims of this one prison in Andersonville, more than seven hundred served in Michigan regiments. I may be pardoned the personal allusion if I say that sixty-three of them served in the same regiment of Michigan volunteers to which I, myself, belonged. Six of them were of those who enlisted in the troop of cavalry which I took away from home to Virginia in the closing month of 1862. One of them was Corporal Hart.

He was an employe of my father. When I came home from the
University in Ann Arbor at the age of twenty-two to raise a
troop of cavalry, he deserted his employer and went with me.
He was a good soldier, a true man and fast friend. He was
captured in one of those skirmishes in Virginia after the battle
of Gettysburg, and reported "missing in action." I never
learned his fate until the other day in looking over the records
in Lansing I found that he died and was buried here. May he
rest in peace. It was forty years ago, but this day the eye will
moisten as memory bridges the years that separate then from
now.

It is a far cry from Michigan to Georgia, but Michigan will
not forget or cease to honor the men who filled the ranks of
her volunteers. Ninety-two thousand of her sons kept step to
the music of the union. Five splendid regiments went out in
the Spanish war and the earnest desire of them all was to be
permitted to serve under that gallant soldier of the south. Fitzhugh Lee, of Virginia. If all those who earned the right to be
listed with the immortals, were to have their names registered
in the hall of fame, Michigan would hold an honorable place.
We recall with pride the names of Williams, Richardson, Poe,
Fairbanks, Brodhead, Town, Roberts, Champlin, Welch, With-
ington, I. C. Smith, Brewer, Snyder, Buhl, Weber, Jewett, the
two Grangers, Finney, and many others whose valor has never
been surpassed.

It was fifty years after the formation of the constitution before Michigan was admitted to the sisterhood of states. Her
pioneers were mostly from New York and New England with a
fair sprinkling from the middle and border states. The first
governor was a son of the south. They were a hardy race of
men, deeply imbuded with the principles that inspired the
colonists in their revolt against the king; with a profound faith
in the destiny of the republic; an intense love of freedom and
loyalty to the union. The first experience her people had in

the duties of federal citizenship came at a time when the sectional disputes that had been smothered by the compromise of the constitution were beginning to manifest themselves. The rumblings of the storm that was brewing between the states were already heard in the political heavens. Andrew Jackson was president. The doctrine that the constitution was a compact between sovereign states had been proclaimed by John C. Calhoun, who maintained the right of the states to nullify a federal statute or to secede from the union. Daniel Webster had appeared as the champion of the union, and its indissolubility. Lewis Cass, who was Secretary of War in Jackson's cabinet, like his chief, stoutly opposed the nullification ideas of South Carolina statesmen. His influence in Michigan, of which state he was a distinguished citizen, was a most potent factor in encouraging and strengthening the sentiment of nationality, as distinguished from that of state sovereignty, which never ceased to dominate the minds of the people of all parties. In the inevitable conflict which followed, and which ended in the appeal to arms,—the only appeal that was possible,—the position of Michigan was never in doubt. Mr. Cass, who was Secretary of State in Buchanan's cabinet, who had been the democratic candidate for president in 1848, and who was as ripe in statesmanship as he was unswerving in his patriotism, Cass resigned his position when Buchanan refused to reinforce Fort Sumter, and came home to encourage enlistments under Lincoln's call for troops. There were no politics in Michigan after the flash of the first gun fired at a federal fort. The colonel of the first regiment of cavalry raised in the State was a democrat, and General Cass was present and made a speech of approval and encouragement when Col. Brodhead mustered his command for the march to Washington. Brodhead was killed at the head of his regiment in a charge at the second battle of Bull Run, the next year. Cass did not long survive the close of hostilities, but his name and that of Thornton F. Brodhead will always be conspicuous in the annals of our State. They were typical "Wolverines."

I repeat, therefore, it is fitting and proper that these distinguished representatives should be here to do honor to the men who helped to keep Michigan in the roll of states which during all these seventy years,—on the rostrum, in the halls of legislation, in the cabinet,—have never failed to stand for the principles of free government, and nationality; or to defend them on the field of battle when called upon to do so. The governor, himself, a veteran of the Civil War, his wife, whose good deeds and exalted character have made her name a household word in Michigan; honorable members of the Senate and House of Representatives, members of the Michigan monument commission; civil and military officials and others high in the councils of the State have come to participate in this ceremony, acting on behalf of all the people of the two peninsulas of Michigan.

It is to me a high honor and a privilege to be selected to say the few words that may be spoken on this occasion. We have come with no bitterness in our hearts on account of those things which were done in that cruel and fraticidal strife of forty years ago. We are met to extend the hand of fraternal greeting to all those, if any there be, who wore the gray and are here present. We remember with pride the part that Georgia played in the revolution. We are familiar with her record in the constitutional convention. We know that she was one of the original states. We have learned that she was one of the three states which cast a unanimous vote for ratification; and the fourth in order to sign the compact by which her statehood was merged in the federal union. It was fate and the fortune of war that brought Michigan and Georgia upon opposing sides in the great conflict of arms which was foreordained by the action of the Fathers. Their soldiers met on many hard fought

RHODE ISLAND MONUMENT, PRISON PARK

PENNSYLVANIA MONUMENT, PRISON PARK.

fields. They learned to know each other's courage to respect
each other's fortitude. They are types of the federal and confederate, the blue and the gray, the "Yank" and the "Reb,"
wherever found. They are no longer enemies. Time has
softened the asperities which civil war engendered. The Spanish War ended all that. Six years ago the people of this country of all sections united in a war to maintain the right of all
men to life liberty and the pursuit of happiness. Even the lust
for wealth, which has done so much to disfigure our national
character, surrendered to a spirit of patriotism,—the love of
money to the love of country. Party rancor ran away. Sectional lines were wiped off the map. There was, as there is today, when the honor of the nation is challenged, no north, no
south, no east, no west; no democrat, no republican, only one
broad sentiment of nationality, as universal as it was unexampled. The people of this great country demonstrated their
unselfish love of justice by making sacrifices for an alien people. Federal and confederate touched elbows under the stars
and stripes. Fitzhugh Lee and "Joe" Wheeler, with commis-
sions from a republican president who fought against them in
the Civil War, engaged in generous rivalry with Merritt and
Wilson to see which could best prove his loyalty to the old flag.
They were all moved by the spirit of Patrick Henry when he
said in the Continental Congress: "I am no longer a Virginian;
I am an American."

Ah, what a spectacle was that, my countrymen! All the
nations of Europe looked on with admiration, albeit alloyed
with envy, at the splendid poise of our president, and the sturdy
purpose of our people. The American soldier and the American sailor made a new record for American valor and American manhood. That war taught not only Spain, but the
world, that business men can handle heavy ordnance; that this
is the most united nation upon the earth; and that even Ameri-

can millionaires have the hearts of patriots, whose blood is not too thick to keep them from fighting when their country needs their services.

Inspired by these thoughts and by the noble words of Mc-Kinley, who said here in Georgia that the time had come for decorating the graves of both federal and confederate soldiers, all alike types of Americanism, your orator avows, and I know that I voice the sentiment of all the people of Michigan, that he is here to preach the gospel of peace and good will, and not the gospel of hate. On the eleventh day of June, 1864, in the battle of Trevillian Station, Virginia, an officer of the 7th Georgia Cavalry surrendered and gave up his arms to me. If he be living, it would be a genuine pleasure for me to meet him and extend the hand of friendly greeting; if he be dead, could I but find it, I would take pride and consider it a privilege to decorate with flowers the grave of my adversary of the war time, whom I met for the first and only time, at the front and upon the skirmish line.

This, my countrymen, may be mere sentiment. It may not. If it be, it is rooted in the soil of a new nation—a nation unified and exalted as it has come to know itself. The old has passed away and the new is in its place. Coincident with the dawning of the twentieth century the United States entered upon a new era of progress and potentiality among the peoples. For the past few years this nation has been making history faster than ever before. It has been an epoch making period in the career of the republic. Only the wisest and most far-seeing statesmanship can catch a glimpse of the possibilities for growth and commanding influence in the world that are concealed in the womb of the future. You who live today are fortunate, for you will be the envy of all lands until the record of the achievements of this people shall have been blotted out from the record of human affairs and forgotten.

How different in the retrospect appears the war of 1861-65

from the war with Spain in 1898. In one, at each other's throats; in the other, at each other's elbows; in that, split into belligerent factions; in this, of one heart and of one mind; in that, trying to pull down "Old Glory"; in this, unitedly seeking to plant it on the mountain peaks where all the world could see it; then warring states; now, a united nation.

The Civil War was one of those crises in human affairs which had to be. The constitution was a compromise. But for those compromises there would have been no union and no constitution. They were necessary to bring the states into the "compact." As it was, two of the states, North Carolina and Rhode Island, held aloof for a long time. But in these concessions for the sake of present good were contained the germs of future dissensions and an irrepressible conflict between two irreconcilable principles. War was from the beginning inevitable. The bond that bound the states together was aptly likened to a rope of sand. The cement that united them was melted by the heats engendered in a presidential campaign, as the mountain snow is melted by the morning sun. Daniel Webster foresaw it and predicted it. But, like Cassandra, he uttered his prophesies to unbelieving ears. When the storm burst, the men of the north and the men of the south were arrayed against each other, in obedience to an inexorable fate, a law as immutable as that which holds the stars in their courses. The time had come when those questions that were postponed by the convention of 1787, had to be settled. There was no way to settle them except by the appeal to arms—the final resort of all nations, in all ages since history began. It took four years to settle them, but they were settled right, and for all time. The war itself was the old story of the red rose and the white rose over again. It was north against south, state against state, section against section, brother against brother, friend against friend.

The time has not yet come—it may never come—when the

stars and stripes and the stars and bars can be blended in a
single national emblem as the crosses of St. George and St.
Andrew are combined in the union jack of England; or as the
white and red roses were united in the standard of Henry VII;
but the men who marched with Grant and with Lee under those
two flags, are today friends and brothers who meet under one
flag and acknowledge allegiance to but one government. In
France, there is still a dispute as to whether the tricolor, the
child of the revolution, or the white flag of the Bourbons, is the
proper national emblem, but in the United States, "Old Glory"
is now undisputed in its right to wave "over the land (the
whole land from ocean to ocean, from gulf to great lakes) of
the free and the home of the brave."

"War is hell," but war has its uses. Far be it from my purpose to palliate the horrors of war. It is a terrible thing. It
is a bitter panacea for human ills, but a panacea still. There
are for the individual worse things than death; so there are for
peoples, things worse than war. (It is better to be dead than
to be in State's prison; one would rather die than to be "Dr.
Jekyll" transformed into "Mr. Hyde.") The age of universal peace, when swords shall be beaten into ploughshares,
spears into pruning hooks; and nation shall not lift up sword
against nation any more; when all international disputes shall
be submitted to The Hague tribunal, has not yet come. Pend-
ing the millennium, the student of history will still judge of the
future by the past. Strange as it might seem, the advance-
ment of the world in civilization, in the arts, in Christianity
itself, has been brought about in a large part by the sword.
Mahomet, with the sword of Islam, for six centuries kept learning from perishing from the earth. Charles Martel drove back
the crescent and set up the cross in Europe. The wars of the
crusades brought about international intercourse and com-
mercial prosperity. The revolt of the barons gave us Magna
Charta; the English revolution parliamentary privilege; the

French and American revolutions liberty. The thirty years' war gave Europe religious toleration. The Franco-Prussian war was necessary to expose the rottenness of the Napoleonic regime and open the way for republicanism in France; if, indeed, the people of our sister republic will ever be able to overcome the blighting influence of centuries of Bourbonism.

These are but a few of the pertinent illustrations which might readily be drawn from history, ancient and modern alike.

War has done much to develop national character. It changed the ferocity of Marat, Danton, and Robespierre, to the heriosm of Massena and Ney—the ferocity of the revolution to the heriosm of Marengo. The Anglo-Saxon, the highest type yet produced, is the result of the mixture of races brought about by war.

And what war has accomplished for national character it has done for individual character also. There are no higher types of men than are to be found among those who fill the ranks and man the ships of our armies and navies. Why are the names of Dewey and Chaffee, today, symbols of all that is lofty in character and glorious in achievement,—one day unknown, the next household words? Why is it?

But to return to the point from which I started upon these digressions—this monument and these men who rest here, in whose memory it was erected:

Whittier once said that the world has not yet outlived its need of symbolism. Monuments, statues, memorial halls, are object lessons, to old and young alike, to this generation not only, but to generations yet to come. The ancients speak to us through their inscriptions on monoliths, pyramids, temples, statues, not less than through their literatures. The civilization of the twentieth century is given symbolic expression in the white city at St. Louis, a triumph of art and architecture, in commemoration of that great event in American history, the Louisiana purchase. The splendid temples and cathedrals which dot the earth from east to west—the occident or the orient—are the visible symbols of mankind's faith, hope, and belief in an overruling God.

In similar language the world has put into permanent and concrete form its admiration for noble and heroic deeds and exalted character. This monument is placed here to be a perpetual sign of Michigan's appreciation of the sacrifices made by Michigan's sons who are buried here, and who are types of all those who met a similar fate here or elsewhere within the borders of these states.

In all ages the mind of man has conceived of valor as closely allied to virtue. In the Roman tongue the same word stood for both. To be virtuous was to be brave. The hero in war was idealized, sometimes deified, and the mythological hero became the mythical god. Sculptors and architects employed their best gifts in designing suitable memorials in his honor. Today, not less than two thousand years ago, virtue is valor. To be brave is not merely to manifest the absence of physical fear in the presence of danger. It is that, but it is much more. It is to exhibit that moral courage which dares to do right under any and all circumstances, in peace not less than in war; knowing your rights to maintain them; to fight, to die for them, if need be. "Fear not death, fear dishonor," was the injunction which the grand master gave the medieval knight who had just taken the oath binding him to the profession of arms. That sentiment, rooted in the soil of chivalry, has grown with the growth and strengthened with the strength of our civilization, until today, as in the past, we find in the soldiers who are educated and trained to fight the battles of their country, types of manhood and citizenship than whom there are and can be none higher. The education of the soldier teaches him to be brave, true, manly, knightly, virtuous; and he holds his life lightly in the scale as against the honor of his country or his own integrity. To be worthy of the designation, "An officer and a gen-

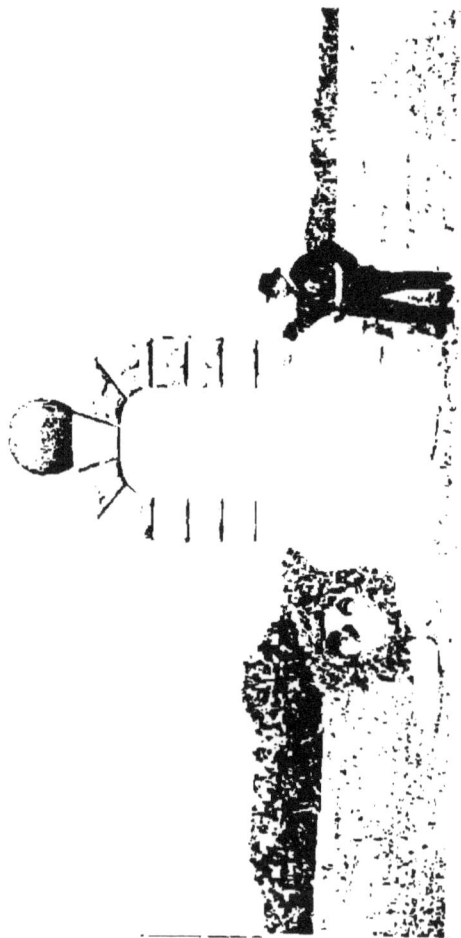

MASSACHUSETTS MONUMENT, PRISON PARK

tleman," is to be immune from the weaknesses and the vices that so often warp the moral fibre of a man. The men of real worth are those who prefer death to dishonor. Of such a breed were the men who fought on both sides in the Civil War, and it is in honor of those who illustrate that higher type of manhood that we are here today.

Who were they?

From first to last more than twenty-six hundred thousand men were enrolled on the union side alone. Of these ninety-two thousand went from Michigan. A quarter of a million sealed with their lives their devotion to the cause for which they fought. Twelve thousand of them and upwards were buried here. They were for the most part young men. They were volunteers, only one in twenty-six a drafted man or a substitute. They came from all the walks of life. The pale-faced student left his Homer to help make the materials for a new epic grander than the Iliad. The merchant exchanged the yard stick for the musket. The bookkeeper abandoned the desk for the drill-ground. The editor gave up the pen for the sword. The teacher parted with the pupils, the preacher with his charge. The farmer went from his half turned furrow, the mechanic from his bench. Doctors dropped their pill-bags, lawyers their briefs. Mothers urged their sons into the ranks, wives their husbands, with fervent blessings and prayers for their safe return. Boys wept if refused the privilege of going as drummer boys, if not bearing arms. Most of them had not the incentive of rank but were common soldiers, privates in the ranks, receiving a paltry stipend as their recompense for risking their lives; for braving disease, enduring hardships, severing the ties at home, relinquishing life's plans and ambitions. The green earth never resounded to the tread of a more heroic body of soldiery than were the volunteers of 1861. They were not soldiers by profession but citizens in arms for a cause. The uniform they wore was a symbol of their fealty to their convic-

tions of right. They held aloft freedom's emblem, not for their
own glory, but for freedom's sake. They knew no guide of
conduct but adherence to the right, as God gave them to see the
right. When their devotion shall be forgotten then, indeed,
will freedom perish from the earth. "The nation that could be
unmindful of such service, would be unworthy to be served by
heroes."

One of these there was. I knew him well, a type of the
American volunteer; well born, of breeding the best; carefully
nurtured in his youth, and trained in that best of all schools, a
happy home. He was of disposition sunny, of manners gentle,
yet of a mental vigor and robust masculinity that made him a
force among his fellows. A model of manly beauty, he might
have posed for a statue of the youthful Apollo. In his cheek
the ruddy hue of health, his bright eye the mirror of a beautiful
life and character, his thoughts were pure as those of any girl.

"A combination and a form, indeed,
Where every god did seem to set his seal
To give the world assurance of a man."

He was young—just turned twenty-one—a student, ambitious,
diligent, intent, alert, bent on carving out for himself a useful
career—an honorable manhood. Study of the noblest antique
types had filled his mind with lofty ideals. Love of native land
was a passion deep-seated in his ardent nature. To him patriotism was the supreme duty of a citizen. The call to arms thrilled
him like an electric shock. His choice was quickly made. Life
plans were abandoned. "Good-bye, old boy," he gaily cried, as
he rushed into the room, one day, and threw his books upon the
table. "I have accepted a position as high private in the rear
rank, and am away to war."

Thus he bade farewell to books, room-mate, home and
marched away. I saw the tear start and the quivering lip as he
pressed for the last time the hand of her who gave him birth;

the tender adieu with her to whom his troth was plighted; the
wistful gaze he cast upon his home as it faded from sight in the
swirl and dust of the departing train; his proud step and military bearing; his diligence and devotion in camp; upon the
march; his alert and vigilant watch upon the picket line; the
intelligence and zeal with which he mastered tactics and the
manifold routine of a soldier's life; the resolute front with
which he marched into his first battle. I saw him in the hospital
when with pale face he tossed in the delirium of fever; on the
transport, disfigured so his own mother could scarce have
known him, by a wound received in battle; and I saw him rush
into the thickest of the fight, seeking death, upon the Rummel
fields at Gettysburg. I saw him tired and ill after many days
and nights of weary marching, yet resolutely and patiently
keeping along in his line of duty. I saw him a wreck of his
former self when he came back exchanged from Andersonville;
and I saw him when with health but partially restored, he re-
joined his regiment to share the dangers of the final campaign.

Only once again I saw him, and he lay insensible to all
earthly hopes and fears in front of the breastworks at Sailor's
creek. Grant had broken through the intrenchments at Peters-
burg; Sheridan's cavalry, headed by the intrepid Custer, was
engaged in a death grapple with the fiery John B. Gordon and
the heroic Fitzhugh Lee, while the lines of both armies swept
on towards Appomattox. But our hero heard it not. His
ear was deaf to the sounds of the tumult. In almost the last
charge of the war, in the moment of final victory, his spirit had
taken its flight. He died breathing a prayer for success, with
the shriek of shell, the ping of bullet, and the thunder of charg-
ing horse for his requiem. His pale ashes were borne by
friendly hands to his distant home in the Peninsula state, and
laid beneath his native turf, there to await the resurrection
morn.

If this be an ideal picture, it is truthfully drawn, albeit from more than one model. With slight changes in names and places, it might have been drawn with equal fidelity to the truth from southern models. As there was no state in the north which did not furnish men who came up to the full measure of the ideal portrait which I have painted, so there was no state in the south which did not furnish their counterparts. The portrait is that of the American volunteer—the typical soldier, the ideal hero of all lands.

When the future Michael Angelo of the republic, in the years to come, far from the passions and prejudices of the present, shall seek to embody in bronze or marble a presentment of the noblest type of manhood that has been produced in this country,—or in any country,—he will set up in the hall of fame a statue, in which all the lines of beauty and of grace in the human figure will be perfectly represented, while its idealized countenance will be illuminated with the majesty and the heroic grandeur of the character of the American volunteer. And there may it stand forever, unique and grand, a perpetual reminder of all that is noblest and best in the long history of the achievements of men.

After the exercises the train was boarded and run to Macon for supper; the next morning to Atlanta, where we were most hospitably received and thence to Chattanooga, where those desiring, visited the battle fields and ascended Lookout Mountain. From there without further delay or stops, the train arrived safely in Detroit Thursday evening.

The last meeting of the commission was held on the train at Troy, Ohio, all members of the commission present. The monument was formally accepted by unanimous vote and $5,500.00 paid the Lloyd Brothers Company. The Lloyd Brothers deserve all credit for their work. The monument is far more beautiful than the drawing of the design—the granite of the purest quality and the workmanship gives evidence of the high-

PROVIDENCE SPRING PAVILION IN ANDERSONVILLE PRISON PARK.

est artistic merit. In the face of many drawbacks, unavoidable delays and a winter of unusual severity, the Lloyds had the monument completed and ready to unveil on time. The Commission expressed their appreciation of their great ability and diligence by the following letter mailed the firm immediately after the return from unveiling the monument:

June 3rd, 1904.

Lloyd Brothers Co.,
                Toledo, Ohio.

Gentlemen:—The undersigned desire to express to you our perfect and entire satisfaction with the manner in which you have performed your contract in erecting the monument at Andersonville, Georgia, to Michigan soldiers and sailors who were imprisoned there during the war of the Rebellion.

From among the numerous designs submitted to this commission the one selected and which we dedicated May 30th is a work of art, classical, ornate and grand. We feared the structure would not equal in beauty the design as shown us; but we are pleased to say that the complete work excels the picture; the granite is of the purest; the carving, caulking, and workmanship of the finest and without a flaw: the whole reflecting infinite credit on its designer, artist and constructor.

We also wish to express our thanks for your universal courtesy and the promptness with which the work has been done.

(Signed.)   E. S. JAMESON,
                G. W. STONE,
                JENNIE CARPENTER.

Michigan Andersonville Monument Commission.

STATEMENT OF ENTIRE RECEIPTS AND EXPENDITURES.

```
To total amount of appropriation.................$6,000.00
By paid for traveling expenses.......... $288.75
By paid for postage....................  12.98
By paid for printing and stationery......  25.25
By paid for speaker stand..............  10.00
By paid for monument................. 5,500.00    5,836.98
                                                 ─────────
      Balance turned back to State Treasurer.......... $163.02
```

The thanks of the commission is gratefully given to Mr. E. S. Past, Superintendent of the National Cemetery at Andersonville, for his courtesy in attending to the preparations for the unveiling ceremonies. also to Comrade Turner in charge of the old stockade grounds for his many kindnesses to the president when visiting the place. also to his care of our party. on the day of the dedication. All the railroad officials vied with each other to make our trip a pleasant and memorable one.

And now in conclusion, to you, Governor Bliss. we wish to extend our sincere thanks for the high honor conferred upon us in appointing us for this very agreeable duty. Our relations have been most harmonious, all having striven to accomplish the object for which we were chosen in a manner for the best interests of our State and it is with a feeling of no little pride that we gazed upon our beautiful monument and felt that we could justly say: "Our labor has not been in vain."

All of which is most respectfully submitted.

(Signed.)   EDWARD S. JAMESON, President.

GEORGE W. STONE, Secretary.

JENNIE CARPENTER, Treasurer.

Michigan Andersonville Monument Commission.

SUPPLEMENTARY.

The commission feel that a tribute of respect is due to that grand organization, the Woman's Relief Corps, for their devoted work in buying the old Stockade and adjacent forts and guard camps that they shall be preserved for all time to our land.

Two states, New Jersey and Pennsylvania, have erected their monuments in the cemetery. Ohio, Rhode Island, Massachusetts and Michigan have placed theirs in what we consider the more fitting spot, in the old prison pen, where our poor boys suffered such exquisite tortures as would have shamed Nero or the Spanish Inquisition. We also felt that the monument should be erected to those who suffered there and perhaps came out alive, as well as to those who had a happy release from their miseries and now lie in peaceful rest beneath the shade in the beautiful cemetery. Our stone is therfore inscribed to all Michigan soldiers and sailors who were imprisoned in these grounds.

Very few know to whom our country is indebted for the knowledge of where our dead lie in the cemetery. Dorence Atwater, a Connecticut soldier and prisoner was the man who at great risk and immense physical labor, got the name, regiment and company of each naked body as it was brought out of the "Old South Gate" every morning, saw the bodies placed side by side in the trenches (about a foot deep) and a number corresponding to the name placed at each man's head. When the death rate was 150 per day, as in August and September, 1864, this must have been very arduous work and how well it was done the figures attest—only about 700 unknown graves out of over 13,000. That this number falls far below the actual deaths there we now know to a certainty. The pen is filled with bones of those who perhaps crawled into a hole

which caved on one too weak to extricate himself. Many
were smothered in tunnels which the poor wretches were constantly digging in hopes of escape—a skeleton was found in
laying the foundation of the Ohio monument and two in ex-
cavating for the Michigan stone.

As soon as Dorence Atwater's record of deaths were published, in July, 1865, Clara Barton got permission of the Sec-
reary of War and taking a large force of carpenters and painters and lumber, while the grave marks were yet visible, erected
a wooden headboard inscribed with the name, company and
regiment at each grave. These have since been replaced with a
marble slab by the government.

We think we cannot do better than to publish in his own
words, Dorence Atwater's account of how he was used and the
reward he received for his work. But for him, but few graves
would ever have been identified. The following was printed as
a preface to the list of dead published by the New York Tri-
bune, but now out of print.

THE DEAD AT ANDERSONVILLE.

INTRODUCTION.

BY DORENCE ATWATER.

To the surviving relatives and friends of the Martyred "Dead" at Andersonville, Georgia:

This record was originally copied for you because I feared that neither you nor the government of the United States would ever otherwise learn the fate of your loved ones whom I saw daily lying before me. I could do nothing for them, but I resolved that I would at least try to let you sometime know when and how they died. This at last I am now able to do.

So many conflicting rumors have been in circulation in regard to these rolls and myself, that I deem it prudent to give a brief statement of my entire connection with this Death Register, and to show how and why it has been so long withheld from you.

On the 7th day of July, 1863, I was taken prisoner near Hagerstown, Md., and taken to Belle Island, Richmond, Va., via Staunton, where I remained five months. I then went to Smith's Tobacco Factory, Richmond, where I kept the account of supplies received from our Government, and issued to federal prisoners of war. In the latter part of February, 1864, I was sent to Andersonville with a squad of four hundred other prisoners from Belle Island, arriving there on the first day of March. I remained inside the stockade until the middle of May, when I was sent to the hospital. On the fifteenth of June, I was paroled and detailed as a clerk in Surgeon J. H. White's office, to keep the daily records of death of all federal prisoners of war. I also made monthly and quarterly abstracts of the deaths, the latter one was said to be for the federal government, which I have since learned was never received.

The appaling mortality was such that I suspected that it was
the design of the rebel government to kill and maim our prisoners by exposure and starvation so that they would forever be
unfit for military service and that they withheld these facts.
Accordingly, in the latter part of August, 1864, I began to
secretly copy the entire list of our dead, which I succeeded in
doing, and brought safely through the lines with me in March,
1865. Arriving at Camp Parole, at Annapolis, Md., I learned
that I could not get a furlough on account of my term of service having expired some seven months before. I immediately
wrote to the Secretary of War, asking for a furlough of thirty
days, for the purpose of having my Death Register published
for the relief of the many thousands anxious in regard to the
fate of their dead. Before an answer could have returned, I
received a furlough from the Commandant of the Camp. I
then went to my home in Terryville, Conn., where I was taken
sick the next day after my arrival, which confined me for three
weeks. On the 12th of April, I received a telegram from the
War Department, requesting me to come immediately to Washington and bring my rolls, and if they were found acceptable,
I should be suitably rewarded. I started the next day for
Washington. Arriving there, I went to the War Department,
and learned that the person (Colonel Breck) with whom I was
to make arrangements was absent at the Fort Sumter celebra-
tion. I left my rolls with the chief clerk for safe keeping. In
a day or two Colonel Breck returned, and he informed me that
the Secretary of War had authorized him to pay me three
hundred dollars ($300) for the rolls. I told him that I did not
wish to sell the rolls, that they ought to be published for the
benefit of the friends of the dead, for whom chiefly they had
been copied. He told me that if I went to publish them the
government would confiscate them, that I could have until 9
o'clock the next morning to decide whether I would take the

three hundred dollars or not. The rolls were then in his possession. I told him that if I could have a clerkship in the department which he had described to me, three hundred dollars, and the rolls back again as soon as copied, I should consider it satisfactory. To this he agreed. He then informed me that it would be necessary for me to enlist in the general service in order to get the clerkship. To this I objected, but in no other way was it available, and I accepted. I was then mustered out of my original enlistment, and given permission to visit home, and return for duty by the 1st of June. While in New York in the latter part of May, I telegraphed to Colonel Breck, asking if my rolls were copied, to which I received a reply, "Not yet."

Soon after my arrival in Washington in June, I called on Colonel Breck, and asked the privilege of taking sheets of my rolls out after business hours, to copy and return them the next morning. He said he would have to ask General Townsend's consent. I met him again in a few days, he told me had been unable to see General Townsend. I then wrote to Colonel Breck, asking if he did or did not intend to return my rolls, that I had promised that the rolls should be published for the benefit of the friends of the deceased. He returned my letter indorsed as follows: "I have fully explained the matter to General Townsend, and he says the rolls shall not be copied for any traffic whatever." I had never spoke of trafficking in them: I only wished to give them to the people for whom I had copied them at some personal risk. Nothing more was said in regard to the rolls until after my return from Andersonville in August.

Miss Clara Barton of Washington, D. C., upon learning the condition of the cemetery at Andersonville, and that the graves could be identified, had reported the facts to the Secretary of War, who ordered the necessary arrangements to be made for the marking of the graves. A party charged with this duty left Washington on the 8th day of July, consisting of Miss Clara

Barton, Captain J. M. Moore, myself and forty-two letterers, painters and clerks, arriving at Andersonville on the 25th of July.

Before leaving Washington it was found that the original register, captured by General Wilson, was deficient in one book containing about twenty-four hundred names, and my rolls were sent to supply the deficiency. The original was also found in many places blurred and imperfect, through want of care, and my rolls were frequently needed to aid this defect. They were, therefore, publicly and constantly in the hands of all who had occasion to consult them and so came into my hands in the course of duty. They had been sent to Washington, according to my agreement with Colonel Breck, and were mine, and lawfully in my possession. I proposed to retain them and give them to you as soon as I could. I did not propose to injure anyone, to do anything unlawful or improper with them, much less to traffic or speculate on the information they contained, but I did retain them. When the originals were needed in the Wirz trial at Washington, they and my copy were in my tent when the messenger arrived in Andersonville. He took the original and left my copy.

When we started home I placed these rolls, with my other property, in my trunk, and brought them to Washington. Upon my arrival I reported to Colonel Breck at the War Department. He asked if I knew where my rolls were. I said: "I have them; will you allow me to keep them, now you have them copied here."

He told me. "We might as well come to an understanding about these rolls. This is the last conversation we shall have about them; if you will pay back three hundred dollars you can keep the rolls, otherwise you must return them." I asked him. "If he did not agree to give them back when copied": he said. "Yes, but you were going to set yourself up in business by publishing them, and we do not consider ourselves held to our agreement." I told him, "I had a right to publish them (if he called that setting myself up in business), and it was my duty to do so." I then turned to leave, intending to see Secretary Stanton. He said, "I infer that you do not intend to give up the rolls." I said, "Not yet; I must go further to see about them." He said, "You will go to the 'Old Capitol' if you do not give them up," and then sent for a guard and had me arrested. My room and trunk were searched, but the rolls could not be found. I was then put in the guard house for two days, and then transferred to the "Old Capitol Prison," and in a few days I was arrainged and tried by court-martial on the following charges and specifications:

Charge 1. Conduct prejudicial to good military discipline. 2. Larceny. Specifications in this that Private Dorence Atwater, of the General Service of the United States Army, did seize and unlawfully take from the tent or quarters of J. M. Moore, Assistant Quartermaster United States Army, certain property of the United States then and there in the proper charge and custody of the said Captain J. M. Moore, towit: a certain document, consisting of a list written upon about twenty-four sheets of paper, of federal prisoners of war who had died at Andersonville, Ga., the same having been prepared by said Atwater, while a prisoner of war at said Andersonville, and sold and disposed of by him to the United States for the sum and price of three hundred dollars, and did appropriate and retain the said property to his own use. This, at Andersonville, Ga., on or about the 16th day of August, 1865.

I was convicted and sentenced as follows: To be dishonorably discharged from the United States service, with loss of all pay and allowances now due; to pay a fine of three hundred dollars; to be confined at hard labor for the period of eighteen months, at such place as the Secretary of War may direct; to furnish to the War Department the property specified in the second specification as the property stolen from Captain J. M.

Moore, and stand committed at hard labor until the said fine is paid, and the said stolen property is furnished to the War Department."

On the 26th day of September I arrived at Auburn State Prison, New York, where I remained over two months at hard labor, when I was released under a general pardon of the President of the United States.

I reached New Haven. Conn., on the following day, and learned that the record had not yet been furnished you. I immediately set out preparing it for publication, and have arranged to have it printed and placed within your reach at the cost of the labor of printing and material, having no means by which to defray these expenses myself.

I regret that you have waited so long for information of so much interest to you.

DORENCE ATWATER.

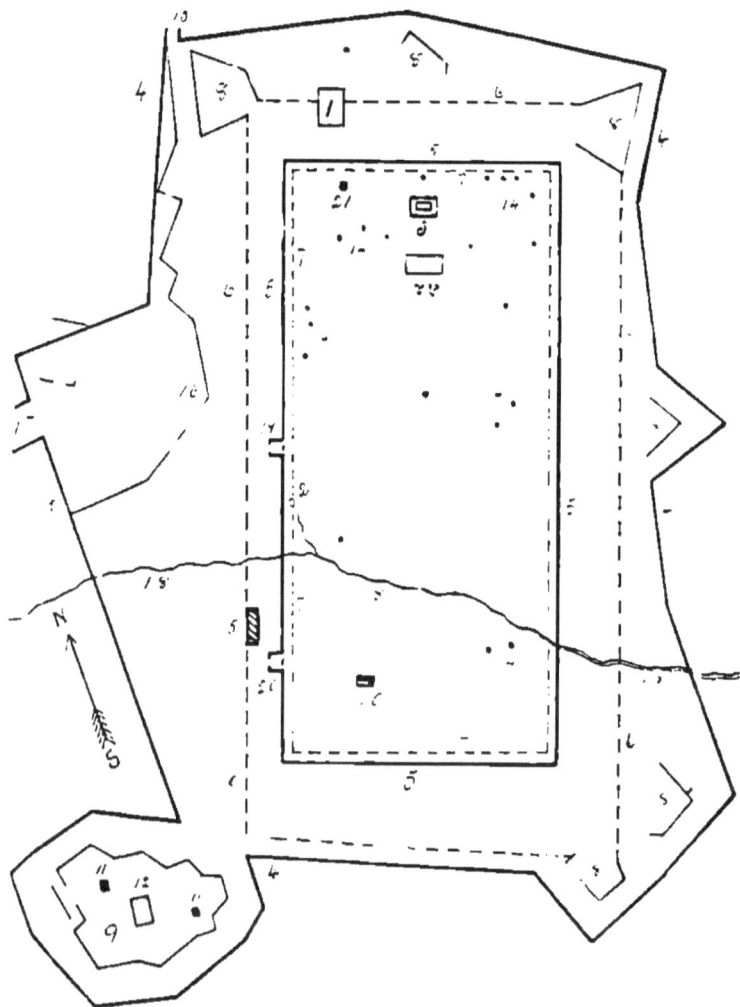

ANDERSONVILLE PRISON PEN.

EXPLANATION:

4. Boundary of Property.
8. Forts and Fortifications.
9, 10, 11, 12. Main Fort.

6. Stockade Proper.
13. Sweet Water Creek.
22. Michigan Monument.

MICHIGAN SOLDIERS IN ANDERSONVILLE NATIONAL CEMETERY.

ANDERSONVILLE, GA., August 13, 1903.

The following list compiled from burial record by

EDWARD S. PAST. *Superintendent.*

No of grave	Name.	Rank.	Company.	Regiment.	Arm of service.	Month.	Day.	Year.
3257	Abbott. C M		E	5	Cav...	July...	13	1864
2247	Acker. James		K	22	Inf....	June..	21	1863
5601	Ackler. W		C	3	Cav...	Aug...	14	1864
12806	Adams. Albert		F	4	" ..	Feb...	7	1864
5472	Alger. Geo		I	10	Inf....	Aug...	13	1864
6713	Allen. Alphonzo		H	14	" ..	" ..	24	1864
12571	Allen. T		A	9	Cav..	Feb...	2	1865
4947	Ammerman. E. H		E	23	Inf....	Aug...	7	1864
2546	Anderson. Geo W		I	23	" ..	June..	27	1864
9156	Anderson. Thos		E	1	Cav .	Sept..	18	1864
12350	Arsnoe. Wm. H		E	7	" ..	Dec...	27	1864
2461	Atkinson. Pat'k		C	22	Inf....	June..	25	1864
6119	Austin. Darius		C	8	Cav..	Aug...	18	1864
6932	Austin. Henry		B	27	Inf....	" ..	27	1864
2198	Ayres. James B	Sergeant.	C	22	" ..	June..	17	1864
2916	Bally. John		M	4	Cav...	July...	3	1864
4610	Baker. Allen		F	5	" ..	Aug...	5	1864
9430	Baker. John		H	1	" ..	Sept..	21	1864
11275	Baldwin. Lewis A		B	24	Inf ...	Oct ...	22	1864
1154	Banghart. John		F	9	Cav...	Apr ...	22	1864
9553	Barber. Uri M	Corporal .	C	26	Inf....	Sept..	21	1864
9553	Barnhard. Geo. W	" .	M	6	Cav..	Oct ...	1	1864
12167	Barnett. T		E	2	" ..	Nov...	28	1864
9477	Bartlett. Emerson H		H	5	Inf....	Sept .	21	1864
2122	Bates. Elijah		E	5	Cav..	June .	17	1864
9850	Batt. William H		L	6	" ..	Sept...	27	1864
3790	Beardslee. Moses A	Sergeant.	D	22	Inf....	July...	50	1864
12130	Beck. George I		H	1	Cav..	Nov...	23	1864
9806	Heckley. Alon		F	10	" ..	Sept .	27	1864
9226	Beckley. Wheeler	Corporal..	E	1	" ..	" ..	19	1864
1511	Heckwith. Edwin	Corporal..	I	6	" ..	May...	31	1864
9705	Beebe. John	" ..	A	1	S. S..	Sept .	20	1864
1681	Beers. Josiah L		E	1	H. A..	June..	6	1864
3591	Benlet. F		A	3	L .A..	July...	19	1864
5970	Bennett. Irwin		G	7	Cav...	Aug...	17	1864
12162	Bennett. Wm. L		G	26	Inf....	Nov...	30	1864
10490	Bentley. Hiram		I	24	" ..	Oct ...	7	1864
2305	Berry. Henry		E	15	" ..	June..	28	1864
5850	Bertaw. J		B	8	Cav..	Aug ..	17	1864
5573	Betts. Randolph		C	1	S. S..	" ..	14	1864
6290	Bibley. Geo		E	9	Cav..	" ..	20	1864
714*	Biers. S		B	18	" ..	" ..	29	1864
727	Billingsly. Joseph		A	1	Batt'y	" ..	29	1864
4109	Billows. John		K	2	" ..	July...	27	1864
4339	Binder. John		A	2	Cav...	" ..	30	1864
3215	Biplx. Jacob C		C	3	" ..	" ..	12	1864
6304	Bircham. Jas. G		B	5	Inf....	Aug...	21	1864
9545	Birdsey. George		B	7	Cav..	Sept..	23	1864
1513	Bishop. Charles		F	27	Inf....	May...	31	1864
10635	Bittman. Jno Jacob		C	1	Cav..	Oct . .	24	1864
10340	Blackburn. C. N		B	5	" ..	Sept...	4	1864
7796	Blair. John		E	7	Inf....	" ..	14	1864
6814	Blanchard. James		F	7	Cav..	" ..	15	1864
3777	Bonmiller. John	Corporal..	H	10	" ..	July...	22	1864
2014	Bostwick. Robert S	" ..	F	2	Inf....	June..	15	1864

MICHIGAN SOLDIERS IN ANDERSONVILLE NATIONAL CEMETERY.—Cont.

No. of grave	Name.	Rank.	Company.	Regiment.	Arm of service.	Month	Day.	Year.
2125	Bowerman, Robert P.......	Corporal..	H	22	Inf....	June..	17	1864
2391	Bowien, John...........		E	27	" ..	" ..	23	1864
1531	Bradley, Geo..........		D	17	" ..	July..	18	1864
7536	Bradley (or Brindley) Benj..		E	9	Cav...	Sept..	1	1864
8505	Bradley, Elmer............	Sergeant	K	11	Inf....	" ..	12	1864
2303	Brigham, David............		D	27	" ..	June..	42	1864
247	Briggs, John..........		E	6	Cav...	" ..	25	1864
3149	Briggs, Wm H..............		G	20	Inf....	July...	11	1864
121	Brockway, Oliver..........	Corporal..	K	11	" ..	Mar...	23	1864
11932	Brotherton, Wm. H........		H	27	" ..	Nov...	9	1864
6865	Brower, Lyman J...........	Corporal..	K	17	" ..	July...	23	1864
1288	Browman, Chs............		H	4	Cav...	June..	30	1864
4395	Brown, Geo W		E	4	" ..	July...	31	1864
9240	Brown, Henry............		A	13	Inf....	Sept..	18	1864
8391	Brown, Henry S...........		F	8	Cav...	" ..	10	1864
8060	Brown, Anderson..........		G	3	Inf....	" ..	15	1864
8333	Brueckleman, Fer'd.......		D	27	" ..	" ..	10	1864
3479	Brunnick, Francis.........		C	3	" ..	July...	17	1864
1517	Brush, John............		K	16	" ..	" ..	18	1864
2301	Bryant, George............		H	6	Cav...	June..	19	1864
5719	Bulsen E F	Sergeant.	....	5	" ..	Aug...	15	1864
9834	Bunker, Rich'd P...........	Corporal..	D	1	Inf....	Sept..	17	1864
6960	Burdick, Theo...........		I	6	Cav...	Aug...	27	1864
6013	Burkhart, Charles..........	Corporal..	G	22	Inf ..	" ..	15	1864
7822	Burr, Wm. W	Sergeant.	L	8	Cav...	Sept..	5	1864
2271	Bush, Thomas J............		A	8	" ..	June..	26	1864
4304	Cahon, Nathan J........		K	1	S S..	Aug...	26	1864
7803	Caldwell, Benjamin........	Corporal..	H	23	Inf...	Sept..	18	1864
12143	Cameron, Francis..........		E	17	" ..	Nov...	24	1864
3565	Cameron, Dan')...........	Sergeant	L	7	Cav...	July...	19	1864
1351	Cameron, John............		H	27	Inf....	May...	25	1864
7534	Campbell, Stephen B........		H	2	" ..	Sept..	1	1864
54	Carpenter, Wm..........		I	2	Cav...	Mar...	17	1864
5005	Carr, Chas. R...........		K	25	Inf....	Aug...	16	1864
3462	Cartney, A.............		E	22	" ..	July...	17	1864
12891	Case, Samuel............	Corporal..	L	3	Cav...	Jan....	4	1865
1164	Castner, John............		L	5	" ..	May...	17	1864
5201	Ceunet, Joseph...........		G	1	" ..	Aug...	10	1864
375	Chambers, Joseph R........	Sergeant.	K	5	" ..	Apr...	5	1864
12834	Chambers, W		G	8	" ..	Feb...	10	1865
1330	Chapman, Horace..........		E	5	" ..	May...	23	1864
210	Chilcote, James C...........		G	20	Inf....	Mar...	28	1864
5696	Churchill, G. W............		C	3	Cav...	Aug...	15	1864
1810	Churchward, Abram R......		C	9	" ..	June..	10	1864
10759	Clags, Stephen...........	Sergeant.	C	7	" ..	Oct....	12	1864
10557	Clark, Rufus W............		H	5	Inf....	" ..	9	1864
1943	Clear, James............		F	22	" ..	June..	14	1864
3143	Clemans, Wm. O............		C	1	S. S...	July...	25	1864
6285	Cobb, G...............		D	4	" ..	Aug...	20	1864
3071	Collins, James...........		I	5	Cav...	July...	9	1864
11743	Collins, Cornelius..........		K	2	Inf...	Nov....	2	1864
2747	Conner, P.............		A	11	" ..	July...	1	1864
1037	Conrad, Edison............		G	8	Inf...	May ..	12	1864
1565	Constantine, John..........		B	9	Cav...	" ..	31	1864
1711	Cook, C...............		D	4	" ..	June..	17	1864
4082	Cook, Jacob..........		H	10	" ..	July...	26	1864
6446	Cook, Geo		H	10	" ..	Aug...	22	1864
11063	Cook, Edward II............		E	6	" ..	Oct....	18	1864
12258	Cook, Nicholas...........		C	1	Inf....	Dec...	10	1864
10644	Cooley, Gilbert............		I	3	" ..	Oct....	11	1864

MICHIGAN SOLDIERS IN ANDERSONVILLE NATIONAL CEMETERY.—*Cont*.

No. of grave	Name.	Rank.	Company.	Regiment.	Arm of service.	Month.	Day.	Year.
837	Coon. Willis S		E	1	S. S...	Sept..	10	1864
4920	Cooper. J. F		F	7	Cav...	Aug..	6	1864
5846	Cope. James P		A	17	Inf....	Sept..	11	1864
6533	Cornell. James		H	7	Cav..	Aug..	23	1864
12474	Covert. E. E		C	6	" ..	Jan...	17	1865
439	Coville. Edwin M		A	7	" ..	Apr...	8	1864
593	Cowell. John		G	6	" "	" ..	17	1864
11582	Cox. William		E	22	Inf....	Oct...	15	1864
10788	Crane. Ralph O		A	17	" ...	" ..	12	1864
1077	Crippen. Geo. F		C	5	Cav...	May.	14	1864
1602	Cronkite. John		K	23	Inf....	June..	7	1864
4620	Cronk. James		G	5	Cav ..	Aug...	3	1864
6263	Cuff. James		F	20	Inf....	" ..	20	1864
3801	Cummings. Willis A		F	2	" ...	July...	22	1864
5688	Cummings. David		I	5	Cav...	Aug.	15	1864
8993	Currie. John D		F	7	" ..	Sept	17	1864
4855	Curtis. Marcus D		C	8	Inf...	" ..	17	1864
9341	Curver. J. H		....	4	Cav...	" ..	20	1864
2617	Cusicks. Byron		C	7	Inf...	June..	18	1864
8651	Dalley. Almerick	Corporal..	F	7	Cav...	Sept .	13	1864
4869	Darce. Wm		K	5	" ..	Aug...	3	1864
1345	Davis. Nelson		E	8	" ..	May...	24	1864
3610	Davy. Rich'd		C	22	Inf....	July...	11	1864
315	Deus. Abraham		L	7	"	Apr...	3	1864
716	Decker. L. A		H	10	Cav...	" ..	24	1864
4690	Decker. Geo. S	Corporal .	K	5	" ..	Aug .	30	1864
43	Deitz. John		I	6	" ..	Mar...	14	1864
5351	Deltall. Wm		A	6	" ..	Aug...	10	1864
2090	Demaree. Dan'l	.....	A	1	Art .	June..	17	1864
195	Demay. John		C	6	Cav..	Mar ..	27	1864
11125	Dennis. Oscar C		H	1	S. S...	Aug...	18	1864
2891	Dennison. Hiram		G	5	Inf ...	June..	30	1864
1286	Denton. Wm. A		E	5	Cav...	May...	23	1864
6401	Denton. Robert A		E	5	" ..	Aug...	29	1864
3619	Deltutt. Francis		C	5	Inf....	July ..	30	1864
1270	Diamond. John		E	27	" ...	May..	21	1864
2240	Dillingham. Wm. O	Corporal..	I	20	" ...	June..	21	1864
10922	Dixon. John		L	5	Cav...	Oct .	14	1864
10161	Doan. Lawrence		L	1	" ..	" ..	1	1864
1292	Dolf. Sylvanus		G	27	Inf....	May...	22	1864
5966	Dolph. S		B	8	" ..	Aug...	14	1864
1193	Dougherty. Daniel		C	8	Cav...	June..	6	1864
3914	Doyle. Wm. C		B	17	Inf....	July...	14	1864
12575	Drake. Orville A		D	27	" ..	Feb...	3	1865
2892	Driscoll. Thomas		H	1	Cav...	July..	4	1864
6225	Drury. Geo		I	5	" ..	Aug...	20	1864
7789	Dumont. W		H	26	Inf....	Sept..	4	1864
12124	Dunroe. Philip T		H	24	" ...	Nov...	22	1864
5070	Dusseau. David Sr.		H	17	" ...	Aug...	8	1864
3267	Dusseau. Oliver		H	17	" ...	July...	12	1864
11734	Dutton. Shubal		C	6	Cav...	Nov...	2	1864
7854	Durfey. Wm. C		H	1	S. S...	Sept..	3	1864
6845	Dyer. James		I	5	Cav...	" ..	29	1864
1210	Eaton. Reuben S		C	27	Inf....	May .	18	1864
1037	Edison. Conrad		G	8	" ..	" ..	12	1864
8855	Edmonds. Byron		H	1	S. S...	Sept	9	1864
7901	Edwards. Seth		E	6	Cav...	" ...	5	1864
8318	Eggleson. Wm. H		C	7	Inf...	July...	5	1864
3081	Elliott. James		G	27	" ..	" ..	20	1864

MICHIGAN SOLDIERS IN ANDERSONVILLE NATIONAL CEMETERY. - Cont.

No. of grave	Name	Rank	Company	Regiment	Arm of service	Month	Day	Year
1240	Ellis, Eugene		B	2	Cav...	May..	20	1864
4501	Emery, Frank N		K	22	Inf ...	July..	23	1864
1104	English, James H		B	17	" ..	Oct..	17	1864
2788	Ensign, Jas H		A	11	" ..	July..	2	1864
2850	Esseltine, Pat'k		K	22	" ...	" ..	15	1864
12065	Evans, Lyman		I	26	" ...	Dec ..	31	1864
2343	Face, W. H		K	6	......	June..	23	1864
5250	Face, Cyrus		B	1	S S...	Sept.	9	1864
2252	Fairbanks, John		G	11	Cav..	June..	21	1864
5081	Farmer, Milton		D	22	Inf ..	Aug..	1	1864
6135	Farnum, Alfred		A	5	Cav...	" ..	19	1864
11265	Fay, Joseph W		G	6	Inf....	Oct ..	21	1864
8560	Feelum, Thomas		G	1	Cav...	May...	1	1864
9557	Finch, Chas E		B	17	...	*Sept.	23	1864
1804	Finchart, David		L	5	Cav...	June..	10	1864
1268	Findlater, Hugh		C	7	...	Feb...	22	1865
4194	Fisher, Theo		C	22	Inf....	July...	30	1864
2197	Fitse, T		C	1	Cav...	June..	19	1864
1064	Fitzpatrick, Matthew		B	1	" ..	May...	13	1864
6983	Fitzpatrick, Matthew		E	8	Inf....	Aug...	27	1864
5881	Flannigan, John		D	5	...	" ..	16	1864
10275	Flinn, Morris		F	27	Inf....	Oct...	3	1864
1367	Folk, John		E	14	" ...	May...	25	1864
7171	Forbes, Carey		B	1	Cav...	Aug...	28	1864
680	Force, Francis		D	27	Inf....	May..	5	1864
10577	Fordhum, Alva		D	1	S S...	Oct.	13	1864
7060	Forsyth, Henry		F	5	Cav...	Aug ..	28	1864
6303	Fox, James		H	3	Inf...	" ..	21	1864
7027	Fox Clark, Sr		B	1	S S.	" ..	27	1861
11709	Fredenburg, Benj. F		E	7	Cav...	Nov...	1	1864
12045	Frederick G		G	9	...	Apr...	23	1865
11800	Freeman, Benjamin		F	1	S S...	Oct...	26	1864
680	Fritscho, Wm		G	22	Inf...	Sept.	15	1864
7659	Gaaf, Jacob		H	17	" ...	" ..	14	1864
12197	Gabrielson, Johannes		F	5	Cav...	Apr...	6	1864
7476	Gaines, Austin		F	22	Inf....	Aug...	3	1864
5718	Gallivan, Michael		I	23	" ...	" ..	15	1864
11207	Gark, James		C	F	Cav	Oct...	20	1864
751	Garly, H		K	1	" ..	Sept..	1	1864
1234	Garrett, Solon H		G	2	" ..	May...	30	1864
2192	Garrigan, John		L	9	" ..	June..	26	1864
1131	Germond, Edward	Corporal	H	13	Inf...	May...	16	1864
10726	Gibbs, Joseph	"	B	7	Cav...	Oct...	11	1864
2925	Gibbons, Mich'l		C	6	" ..	July...	5	1864
7741	Gibson, Jos. L		K	1	S S...	Sept.	3	1864
8312	Gibson, David E		F	23	Inf...	" ..	10	1864
2882	Gilbert Freeman		K	3	" ...	June .	4	1864
10071	Gillett, Lyman		F	22	...	Sept..	28	1864
6866	Gillis, John		F	4	Cav...	Aug...	20	1864
7624	Given, Douglas		I	8	Inf...	Sept..	2	1864
1049	Goubald, Wm		L	2	Cav...	May ..	12	1864
12573	Goodell, M		C	5	...	Feb...	2	1865
145	Goodenough, G. M		K	23	Inf ...	Apr...	14	1864
3803	Goodman, Wm		I	5	Cav...	July.	24	1864
2634	Gordon, James		D	6	" ...	June...	28	1864
11352	Goucher, Thomas		B	6	" ..	Oct...	23	1864
956	Graham, Geo. M		C	5	" ...	May...	5	1864
7968	Grant, A. H		D	7	" ...	Sept..	6	1864
8628	Gray, Geo		M	1	" ...	" ..	13	1864

MICHIGAN SOLDIERS IN ANDERSONVILLE NATIONAL CEMETERY —*Cont·*

No. of grave.	Name.	Rank.	Company.	Regiment.	Arm of service.	Month.	Day.	Year.
11302	Gray, James		E	6	Cav...	Oct...	23	1864
6482	Greek, C. H		K	1	" .	Aug...	26	1864
4225	Green, Edwin A		H	11	Inf..,.	July..	29	1864
4092	Griffin, Geo. S		H	11	" ..	" ..	27	1864
794	Gripman, John		M	5	Cav...	Apr...	28	1864
1927	Grimley, James H		D	22	Inf....	June..	14	1864
566	Grover, James		H	10	Cav...	Apr...	15	1864
11647	Grubaugh, Jacob		G	5	" ..	Oct...	19	1864
5818	Guinan, Bernard S	Sergeant.	K	17	Inf....	Aug...	16	1864
1813	Haines, Riley		G	9	Cav...	June..	10	1864
4674	Hale, Samuel B		D	7	" ..	Aug...	3	1864
6	Hall G E		M	2	" ..(	Mar...	5	1864
5931	Hall, Wm		I	26	Inf....	Aug...	17	1864
11046	Hall, Joseph H		E	1	S. S...	Oct ..	18	1864
12885	Halsall, Davis E		A	8	Cav...	Mar...	27	1864
11260	Hamlin, J. H		K	1	S. S...	Oct...	21	1864
3869	Hance, Chas	Bugler....	D	7	Cav...	July...	24	1864
3927	Hankins, Geo		H	12	....	" ..	25	1864
1452	Hannah, John J		C	22	Inf....	June..	9	1864
3015	Hardy, John D		H	4	" ..	July...	7	1864
9718	Harper, D		E	3	....	Sept...	25	1864
8824	Harrington, Geo. L		L	6	Cav...	" ..	13	1864
847	Hart, Isaac R	Corporal.	E	6	" ..	May...	7	1864
409	Hartsell, George		B	7	" ..	Apr...	6	1864
1910	Harty, J. S		F	16	Inf....	June..	12	1864
9233	Hawley, Chas		F	4	Cav...	Sept .	10	1864
11057	Hayes, James		E	1	....	Oct...	17	1864
5370	Haynes, John		H	1	Cav...	Aug...	11	1864
2660	Hays, Chauncey		H	5	" ..	June..	19	1864
11070	Haywood, James B		H	1	" ..	Oct...	17	1864
4426	Heath, Myron		C	21	Inf....	July...	31	1864
11835	Helmer, Charles		M	6	Cav...	Nov...	5	1864
367	Henry, James		A	8	" ..	Apr...	4	1864
6992	Henry, Austin		B	27	Inf....	Aug...	27	1864
4246	Heron, John	Corporal.	F	5	Cav...	July...	30	1864
1656	Herriman, Daniel		D	22	Inf....	June..	6	1864
6176	Hibler, A	Corporal.	D	9	Cav...	Aug...	20	1864
13612	Hicks, Chas. O		B	8	" ..	Feb...	8	1865
11412	Hill, Wm		A	1	S. S...	Oct...	24	1864
1038	Hoag, Joseph		H	20	Inf....	" ..	4	1864
11386	Hoag, J. M		H	20	" ..	" ..	23	1864
11757	Hodges, Myron G	Sergeant.	I	22	Inf....	Nov.,	3	1864
12740	Hogins And'w		A	4	Cav...	Mar...	6	1865
8100	Holcomb, John		A	6	" ..	Sept ..	6	1864
5332	Holland, George		I	1	" ..	" ..	8	1864
6110	Holmes, James J		H	22	Inf....	Aug...	15	1864
337	Holton, Samuel W		B	1	" ..	Apr...(	2	1864
860	Hood, James D		H	22	" ..	May...	2	1864
5368	Hoover, A		H	1	Cav...	Aug...	11	1864
3286	Hopkins, Nathaniel		E	6	" ..	July...	12	1864
1644	Hough, Martin		D	22	Inf....	June..	13	1864
11503	Houk, Henry L	Corporal.	I	24	" ..	Oct...	28	1864
3483	Housing, Walter L	" ..	C	7	Cav...	July .	17	1864
11400	Howard, Frank S	Sergeant.	E	8	" ..	Oct...	20	1864
12067	Howe, Isaac O		F	7	" ..	Nov...	17	1864
1625	Howell, Leander W		M	1	" ..	June..	5	1864
3040	Hurhey, B		B	17	Inf....	July...	8	1864
6888	Hungerford, Chas, E	Sergeant.	E	20	" ..	Aug...	25	1864
6909	Hunt, L		C	2	....	Aug...	27	1864
1519	Hunter, Florence A		F	22	Inf....	June..	1	1864

MICHIGAN SOLDIERS IN ANDERSONVILLE NATIONAL CEMETERY.—*Cont.*

No. of grave.	Name	Rank.	Company.	Regiment.	Arm of service.	Month.	Day.	Year.
4166	Hunter, Mortimer W	Corporal	F	22	Inf....	July	2	1864
1738	Huntley, H		E	5	Cav...	June..	5	1864
5376	Husted, J		C	10		Aug...	10	1864
818	Hutton, Samuel		G	6	Cav...	Apr..	30	1864
5141	Ingraham, Wm. L		B	5	" ..	Aug...	9	1864
1817	Jackson, James		I	7		June..	10	1864
3621	Jackson, James G		F	22	Inf....	July ..	29	1864
9716	Jackson, Christopher		E	8	Cav...	Sept	25	1864
3564	Jakeway, Ebenezer		B	7		July ..	18	1864
12940	Jamison, Hugh		H	5	"	Nov...	14	1864
4736	Johnson, Jerman H		G	7	"	Aug...	4	1864
657	Johnson, James		I	24	Inf....	"	23	1864
7753	Johnson, Henry		L	7	Cav...	Sept..	3	1864
12461	Johnson, And'w		C	5	"	Oct..	16	1864
2576	Jones, Augustus		E	6	Inf....	June..	27	1864
12886	Jourdron, M		K	1		Jan...	5	1865
7529	Jump, Dallas P		E	1	S. S...	Sept..	1	1864
7164	Keatin, Michael		E	7	Cav...	Aug..	29	1864
487	Keintzler, K		F	5	"	Apr...	11	1864
472	Kendall, Wm. H		D	6	"	Aug...	4	1864
4397	Kennedy, H		H	27	Inf....	July..	31	1864
10790	Kenzal, Geo		B	5	Cav...	Oct...	12	1864
12164	Kepfoot, Louis		E	6	"	Mar...	26	1864
706	Kere, Wm		A	2	Inf....	Apr...	23	1864
8249	Kessler, Jacob		G	11	"	Sept...	9	1864
368	King, Leander		G	8	Cav...	Apr...	1	1864
9251	Kinner, Jesse		C	1	"	Sept...	19	1864
4421	Kinney, John H		H	17	"	July...	31	1864
13431	Kinney, Corwin		H	5	Cav...	Nov...	14	1864
10448	Kirkham, H. C		E	5	"	Oct...	14	1864
7486	Kling, Jacob		K	2	"	Sept..	1	1864
4110	Klunder, Chas. Jr		F	5	"	July...	28	1864
34	Kohn, Fred'k		F	7	Inf....	Mar...	11	1864
7694	Kopp, J. L	Sergeant	K	1	Cav...	Aug...	28	1864
4092	Laduke, James		G	17	Inf....	"	7	1864
3803	Lanning, Harlow B		H	22	"	July...	14	1864
5142	Lark, Edward		F	23	"	Aug...	19	1864
9685	Lard, H. O (unkn on stone)		D	22	"	Sept..	24	1864
5776	Laratee, Lucian D		H	8	Cav...	Aug...	15	1864
5923	Laughlin, Moses E		H	17	Inf....	"	17	1864
6865	Lehman, Gottlieb		H	8	Cav...	Sept ..	7	1864
1187	Lewis, Philander		D	5	"	May..	18	1864
1802	Lewis, F. L	Vet.Surg.		9	"	June..	12	1864
9700	Lind, James		H	6	"	Sept...	25	1864
980	Lorain, John		E	27	Inf....	May...	8	1864
6997	Loru, James	Sergeant	M	3	Cav...	Aug...	24	1864
223	Lossing, Jonathan		B	8	"	Mar.	29	1864
5216	Lowell, James		E	7	"	Aug...	11	1864
1771	Lowze, Peter		D	22	Inf....	June ..	15	1864
4913	Luce, Franklin		A	1	Art...	Aug...	6	1864
12016	Luener, John		F	17	Inf....	Apr ..	21	1864
11808	Lutz, Wm F		F	6	Cav...	Oct...	11	1864
3700	Lyon, Aaron D	Corporal	G	5	"	July...	21	1864
2255	Maby, Edw'd B		K	8	Cav...	June..	21	1864
11511	Mackswaser, W		K	1	S. S...	Oct...	26	1864
208	Maguire, John		A	20	Inf....	Mar..	31	1864
11582	Maher, Daniel		C	27	" ..	Oct...	26	1864

MICHIGAN SOLDIERS IN ANDERSONVILLE NATIONAL CEMETERY.—*Cont.*

No. of grave.	Name.	Rank.	Company.	Regiment.	Arm of service.	Month	Day	Year
3537	Manry, And'w		G	17	Inf....	July...	18	1864
2423	Nanwaring, Wm		D	22	" ...	Aug...	1	1864
9185	Marleu, Wm		E	22	" ...	Sept..	19	1864
542	Markhum, Darius A		B	5	Cav...	July...	14	1864
2976	Marr, Thos G		A	5	Inf....	" ..	7	1864
3090	Marshall, H. E		B	27	" ...	" ..	9	1864
12674	Marshall, Geo. W		N	4	Cav ..	Feb..	19	1865
7513	Mason, Peter		L	7	" ..	Sept..	4	1864
2759	Maxpadder, Wm		E	22	Inf....	" ..	1	1864
10575	Mayo, Thomas		H	6	Cav...	Oct...	9	1864
9750	McArthur, Wallace	Sergeant.	D	7	" ..	Sept .	25	1864
3936	McCabe, Felix		H	22	Inf....	Aug .	15	1864
10690	McCall, Wm		E	20	" ...	Sept .	18	1864
218	McCartney, Hiram		K	6	Cav ..	Mar...	29	1864
6249	McCarty, Chas.		I	26	Inf....	Aug...	18	1864
12252	McCuughn, Wm		B	7	Cav...	Dec...	9	1864
612	McCotter, James		H	27	....	Apr...	18	1864
7473	McCloud, A		I	21	Inf....	Sept...	1	1864
6387	McClure, Ralph		H	7	Cav...	" ..	10	1864
16835	McClury, Wm. H	Corporal.	H	7	" ..	" ..	2	1864
2548	McDowell, J		F	8	" ..	June..	24	1864
4078	McFall, Harrison		E	17	Inf ...	July..	27	1864
10423	McGill, Thomas		A	9	Cav...	Oct...	6	1864
12093	McGraw, John		F	1	S. S...	Nov ...	18	1864
8590	McGinnis, Peter		I	16	Inf....	Apr...	12	1864
8050	McKay, Kennith		G	10	" ..	Sept..,	6	1864
7379	McLane, Thos		I	1	S. S...	Aug...	30	1864
10958	McMillan, Alex		M	5	Cav...	Oct ...	15	1864
12733	McNeill, C		M	8	" ..	Mar...	5	1865
11548	McNimm, Wm. R		A	17	Inf ...	Oct....	27	1864
11536	Melosh, Francis		D	9	Cav...	" ..	27	1864
5430	Mench, Chas	Sergeant.	I	20	Inf....	Aug...	14	1864
5559	Merner, Christian		D	5	" ..	" ..	13	1864
7309	Merrill, Simon B		G	5	" ...	" ..	30	1864
5325	Miller, Herman		A	16	" ..	" ..	11	1864
5153	Miller, L		F	7	" ..	" ..	9	1864
4144	Miller, Joseph		C	5	Cav...	July...	28	1864
1692	Miller, Chas. H. W		D	5	" ..	May...	13	1864
1710	Miller, Joseph		C	3	Inf....	June..	7	1864
3840	Miller, Wesley		K	2	" ..	July...	1	1864
11126	Miller, John A		F	10	" ..	Oct...	18	1864
13085	Miller, Henry		A	9	Cav...	Nov...	15	1864
8518	Mills, Chas. S	Corporal.	F	1	" ..	Sept..	11	1864
5030	Misner, James	"	F	6	" ..	Aug...	17	1864
7916	Monroe, John		I	7	Inf...	Sept..	5	1864
9791	Moon, John H		G	6	Cav...	Nov...	12	1864
7114	Moore, James		B	7	Inf...	Aug...	27	1864
3054	Morgan, Martin C		E	2	Cav...	July...	25	1864
4942	Morgan, E. C		G	23	Inf...	Aug...	7	1864
12458	Morland, J		I	1	....	Jan ...	15	1865
3150	Morris, A. T		K	14	Inf ...	July..	11	1864
8807	Morrison, James		F	21	....	Sept..	16	1864
10134	Morse, Allen		M	8	Cav...	Oct...	1	1864
7918	Morton, Peter		H	17	Inf....	Sept .	5	1864
10011	Moses, Chas. E		I	5	Cav...	" ..	24	1864
8954	Mosher, Stephen		I	7	" ..	" ..	9	1864
4301	Mowry, John		L	5	" ..	July...	30	1864
7962	Mueller, Francis		G	22	Inf...	Aug...	1	1864
1059	Munn, Oliver F		F	27	....	May...	13	1864
4783	Munroe, David A		A	6	Cav...	Aug...	5	1864
8976	Munson, Homer C		E	5	Inf....	Sept..	16	1864

MICHIGAN SOLDIERS IN ANDERSONVILLE NATIONAL CEMETERY.—Cont.

No. of grave.	Name.	Rank.	Company.	Regiment.	Arm of service.	Date of death.		
						Month.	Day.	Year.
8025	Murray, Edwin W.		G	17	Inf....	Sept..	6	1864
7836	Musket, George	Corporal.	K	1	Cav...	" ..	5	1864
6821	Myer, E. L.		I	4	" ..	Aug..	25	1864
6329	Myers, Chas F.		H	6	" ..	Oct...	9	1864
5100	Naugle, C.		G	11	......	Aug .	12	1864
2077	Nash, Charles		H	22	Inf...	June .	17	1864
4402	Neck, N.		K	4	Cav..	July...	27	1864
5392	Neidhamer, Jacob		D	20	Inf...	Aug..	8	1864
5493	Nevarr, Alex		E	17	" ..	....	13	1864
1209	Newberry, James		K	5	Cav..	May...	19	1864
2529	Nicholds, John		A	15	Inf...	July...	3	1864
513	Nicolson, Edwin		G	6	Cav..	Apr	12	1864
1812	Northam, Otheriah F.		M	6	" .	Sept .	26	1864
1005	Nourse, Hiram W.		L	5	" .	May..	10	1864
11011	Noyes, James		E	1	S. S...	Oct...	16	1864
11911	Nyland, Hendrickus.		D	8	Inf..	Aug..	8	1864
12890	Oathout, Delas.		H	18	Inf....	Jan...	1	1865
285	O'Brien, Aus. P.		H	9	Cav...	Apr...	1	1864
8511	O'Brien, Wm. H	Sergeant	A	7	" ..	Sept...	11	1864
9081	Ogden, Edward S.		M	5	" ..	..	17	1864
11940	O'Leary, Jere	Corporal.	H	1	S. S..	Nov...	9	1864
409	Oliver, Alex		G	8	Cav...	Apr...	12	1864
2267	Olney, Geo. W		A	1	Inf...	June..	21	1864
5574	O'Neal, John		K	22	" ..	July..	10	1864
8141	Oomy, Samuel		C	20	" ..	Sept .	8	1864
5846	Orcutt, Corydon		F	3	......	Aug ..	16	1864
1189	Orrison, George..		M	9	Cav..	May..	18	1864
11999	Osborn, Jedediah D		E	6	" ..	Nov...	14	1864
4384	Osborne Stephen A		B	27	Inf....	July..	31	1864
4874	Overmyers, Thos. S		D	6	" ..	Aug...	8	1864
1882	Paisley, Andrew G	Sergeant.	K	22	Inf . .	June.	13	1864
5852	Palmer, Dan'l H		D	5	Cav .	Aug..	6	1864
11177	Palmer, Porter.		H	10	Inf .	Oct ...	19	1864
103?	Parker, Benjamin C	Sergeant	C	8	Cav..	May...	12	1864
7900	Parks, Ira A		E	5	" ..	Sept..	8	1864
7289	Parks, Van Runseler		C	7	" ..	Aug...	30	1864
3501	Parmalee Joseph		C	7	" ..	July ..	19	1864
8195	Parmalee, James	Corporal.	H	23	Inf ..	Sept.	8	1864
13702	Parmelee, Chauncey	" ..	M	8	Cav..	Mar ..	12	1865
1374	Parrish, Thos.		I	8	" ..	May...	28	1864
443	Parsons, Zenas		I	7	" ..	Apr...	9	1864
4255	Payette, Nelson		E	22	Inf....	July...	30	1864
1907	Payne, R H.		I	6	Cav..	June..	15	1864
5546	Peek, James H	Corporal..	D	1	S. S..	Aug...	30	1864
2551	Pfeffer, John		I	6	Cav..	June..	28	1864
5799	Pentecost, Wm. G		E	18	Inf...	Aug...	15	1864
4276	Perigo, John		D	2	Cav..	May..	24	1864
7354	Perrin, N		H	8	" ..	Aug...	31	1864
5715	Pettibone, Salem E		D	7	" ..	" ..	15	1864
4092	Philbrook, F		A	1	Art...	" ..	3	1864
3516	Pierson, Dan'l		C	3	Cav...	July...	18	1864
8836	Pike, Benjamin F	Corporal..	C	2	" ..	Sept...	13	1864
2401	Pitcher, Eugene		H	5	Inf...	July..	3	1864
8086	Plant, Wm		M	7	Cav..	Sept..	16	1864
11046	Platt, Lyman A		A	22	Inf...	" ..	30	1864
12273	Pleus, Wm		C	5	Cav..	Nov....	" ..	1864
5056	Podruff Daniel		B	13	Inf...	Aug...	8	1864
5812	Pond, Chas		L	1	" ...	" ..	14	1864

MICHIGAN SOLDIERS IN ANDERSONVILLE NATIONAL CEMETERY.—*Cont.*

No. of grave.	Name.	Rank.	Company.	Regiment.	Arm of service.	Month.	Day.	Year.
4564	Porter, Levi		C	1	S. S...	Aug..	2	1864
4100	Post, Russell L		H	10	Inf..	July...	27	1864
1257	Pratt, L		C	7	Cav...	Feb ..	3	1865
12109	Preston, James N		C	6	" ..	Jun ..	7	1865
11986	Preston, Benj		F	7	" ..	Nov...	13	1864
2700	Provee, Felix		I	22	Inf ...	July...	30	1864
513	Pullman, Geo		I	5	Cav...	Apr ..	12	1864
11675	Raley, H		L	24	Inf....	Oct...	30	1864
11457	Rumsey, James	Sergeant.	H	5	Cav ..	" ..	25	1864
10860	Randall, Lorenzo D		D	6	Inf....	" ..	5	1864
11705	Recalt, S		K	1	......	Nov...	1	1864
12745	Reeves, Mark		G	15	Inf....	Mar..	8	1865
6154	Relic, Antonio		G	17	" ..	Aug ..	19	1864
7855	Rich, Ansel		B	11	" ..	Sept..	6	1864
4916	Richards, Geo. M		I	16	" ..	Aug..	7	1864
12553	Richardson, Wilford B		L	1	Eng...	Jan .	29	1865
3740	Riggs, Jere		I	27	Inf....	Sept..	21	1864
3742	Riley, Chas		I	6	Cav...	July..	20	1864
8937	Riley, Miles	Corporal..	F	7	" ..	Sept..	13	1864
11151	Riley Rich'd	Sergeant.	H	24	Inf....	Oct...	19	1864
922	Robinson, Wm. H		H	22	" ..	May...	5	1864
7750	Robinson, Henry P		L	5	Cav...	Sept..	3	1864
10136	Robinson, Francis		F	22	Inf....	" ..	2	1864
12540	Rodgers, Wm		G	30	" ..	Feb...	5	1865
77	Rolloff, John		E	5	Cav...	Mar...	30	1864
623	Rolands, Richard		M	6	" ..	Apr...	19	1864
2201	Hollands, Rich'd		M	6	" ..	June..	21	1864
5885	Ronan, John		C	5	" ..	Aug...	16	1864
5176	Rood, Chas. H		C	22	Inf....	" ..	1	1864
2402	Ruggles, Oscar		H	22	" ..	June ..	24	1864
3676	Russ, James		C	22	" ..	July...	23	1864
324	Russell, Peter		G	21	" ..	Apr...	5	1864
7507	Ryan, Wilson		E	1	S. S..	Sept..	1	1864
9614	Ryno, Thaddeus		I	22	Inf...	" ..	30	1864
2259	Sanborn, Horace		K	22	" ..	June..	21	1864
1406	Sanburn, Horace		K	22	" ..	Mar...	27	1864
2051	Sannier, Clement		G	24	" ..	June ..	29	1864
7676	Sateriee, Hiram J		E	6	Cav...	Sept..	3	1864
11508	Sawbecome, Vedan		K	1	S. S...	Oct...	21	1864
7350	Sawyer, James M		G	1	Cav...	Aug...	31	1864
1948	Schaufer, Gottlelb		G	22	Inf....	June ..	20	1864
1732	Schemmerhorn, John		C	7	Cav ..	May...	24	1864
7303	Schimer, Fred K		G	22	Inf....	Aug...	30	1864
752	Schofield, Charles H		G	27	" ..	Sept...	1	1864
3343	Seill, Hilbert	Sergeant.	F	9	Cav...	July...	4	1864
423	Seybert, David S	Corporal.	H	1	S. S...	June .	30	1864
520	Shannon, John		H	20	Inf....	Apr...	13	1864
3951	Sharp, James W		H	6	Cav...	July...	25	1864
2696	Shaw, Francis H		K	2	Inf....	" ..	7	1864
7912	Shaw, Frank G		K	2	" ..	" ..	25	1864
350	Sheldon, Horace S		I	1	Cav...	Apr...	3	1864
10417	Shell, Michael		A	7	Inf....	Oct...	8	1864
3524	Shultz, Chas. I		B	5	Cav...	July...	18	1864
3044	Shunway, Wm		L	8	" ..	" ..	18	1864
3065	Sibley, John E	Sergeant.	G	7	Inf....	" ..	9	1864
11771	Sickles, N		I	14	......	Nov...	3	1864
1289	Simmer, Adolph		H	27	Inf....	Dec...	6	1864
10254	Simmons, Allen F	Sergeant.	E	17	" ..	Oct...	3	1864
6506	Simmonds, Albert O		E	7	Cav...	" ..	3	1864

MICHIGAN SOLDIERS IN ANDERSONVILLE NATIONAL CEMETERY.—Cont.

No. of grave	Name	Rank.	Company	Regiment	Arm of service	Month	Day	Year
10444	Simpson, John P.		A	22	Inf....	Oct...	20	1864
351	Simpson, Enoch T		G	6	"	July..	1	1864
6323	Simpson, Thompson		I	8	"	Aug...	21	1864
172	Smith, Wm		L	7	Cav.	Mar ..	26	1864
812	Smith, Wm W	Corporal..	D	5	"	May..	2	1864
1628	Smith, Lewis F		L	1	"	June..	5	1864
1801	Smith, Silas C		C	17	Inf....	"	10	1864
2507	Smith, Cyrus		E	1	Art...	"	26	1864
4859	Smith, Wm		H	17	Inf....	Aug..	6	1864
12676	Smith, Chas. B		L	8	Cav..	Feb...	20	1865
12801	Smith, Geo.		H	8	" .	Mar..	20	1865
6696	Smoke, Horace B.		H	6	"	Aug...	15	1864
1446	Snow, Levi		H	20	Inf....	May..	2	1864
134	Snyder, Eugene		F	17	" .	Mar...	24	1864
9629	Snyder, John		M	5	Cav.	Sept..	27	1864
236	Soper, Calvin C.		H	27	Inf....	Mar.	14	1864
12310	South, Peter		K	1	S. S...	Dec...	27	1864
10117	Spencer, Geo		H	21	Inf..	Oct...	1	1864
10285	Spencer, John		I	2	"	"	4	1864
2807	Sprague, Napoleon B		I	11	Inf....	July...	3	1864
4311	Sprague, Benj.		D	7	Cav..	"	30	1864
11510	Springer, Joseph		A	7	"	Oct...	8	1864
12223	Sprowles, Conrad		H	1	"	Dec...	5	1864
8560	Staning, G. W	Corporal..	G	5	Art.	Sept..	12	1864
12361	Stedman, Stephen P		H	10	Cav..	Oct...	31	1864
3401	Steele, E	Sergeant.	C	2	"	July...	7	1864
1741	Stevens, Seneca	Corporal..	K	22	Inf....	June..	"	1864
2604	Stevens, L		M	6	Cav	"	20	1864
9481	Stewart, Wm V	Sergeant.	E	5	"	Sept..	21	1864
9469	Stewart, Francis		E	6	"	"	21	1864
854	Stillwell, Lyman D		M	6	"	May...	3	1864
4103	Stines, H	Corporal..	K	4	"	July...	27	1864
11351	Stoddard, Silas		D	5	Inf....	Oct...	23	1864
5972	Stowe, Geo		C	10	" .	Aug...	17	1864
13090	Straub, C. Adam		F	5	Cav...	Sept..	30	1864
1805	Strickland, Thomas		E	10	Inf...	June..	14	1864
12254	Strickner, J		D	16	" .	Dec ..	10	1864
2865	Stuart, Clark A		F	7	Cav..	June..	30	1864
3253	Stubbs, James		L	6	" .	July...	15	1864
1082	Stuck, Lyman H		B	2	Inf....	May...	14	1864
7014	Sullivan, John		E	27	" .	Aug...	27	1864
8000	Sutherland, Jerman		A	5	Cav...	Sept..	6	1864
8100	Surphin, Horace		F	10	Inf....	"	1	1864
11234	Sutton, Henry		I	22	" .	"	30	1864
5193	Swain, Darwin P		A	6	Cav...	Aug...	9	1864
11130	Swart, Martin W		E	3	Inf....	Oct...	10	1864
1301	Tancred, Mathew		B	14	" .	May...	25	1864
9103	Taylor, N		F	22	" .	Sept..	1	1864
1111	Taylor, Jared M		A	11	" .	Oct...	1	1864
1301	Terrell, Henry		H	22	" .	May...	31	1864
9331	Thanet, Wm		D	22	" .	July...	15	1864
3494	Thatcher, Elizar H		F	6	Cav...	"	1	1864
6703	Thompkins, Nathan R		B	1	S. S..	Aug...	21	1864
7544	Thompson, Wm H		F	8	Cav	"	23	1864
7797	Thompson, Marcus C		I	5	" .	Sept..	4	1864
7600	Tift, Horace M		M	5	"	Aug...	27	1864
12629	Till, Geo		B	2	"	May..	24	1864
923	Tindall, Wm		B	11	Inf...	Sept..	21	1864
4433	Tols, Thomas		G	17	" .	July...	31	1864
7593	Tracy, David		M	7	Cav...	Sept..	2	1864

MICHIGAN SOLDIERS IN ANDERSONVILLE NATIONAL CEMETERY.—*Cont.*

No. of grave.	Name.	Rank.	Company	Regiment.	Arm of service.	Month.	Day.	Year.
						Date of death.		
2945	Tubbs. Philip		K	7	Cav.	July...	6	1864
12050	Tuly, Harvey H		H	6	"	Nov...	15	1864
1114N	Twisler. C	Sergeant.	K	5		Oct...	10	1864
3945	Udell. W. O (stone marked for unknown)		D	2		July...	23	1864
12166	Van Allen. Cicero D		K	27	Inf	Nov...	26	1864
935N	Vanukin. Francis		G	16	"	Sept..	17	1864
2094	Vau Brunt. Wm. H		E	9	Cav	July...	7	1864
731	Vunderhoff. James		G	6	"	Apr...	23	1864
2270	Van Dyke, John T		D	6	"	June..	20	1864
1126	Van Gleson. Lewis	Sergeant.	D	5	"	May...	13	1864
327N	Vanliew. Cornelius	"	F	6	"	July...	14	1864
644	Van Scotan. Wm. H		K	6	"	Aug..	1N	1861
7595	Van Sickle. Lyman	Sergeant.	G	5	"	"	31	1864
10044	Varney. Horace A		D	17	Inf.	Sept...	29	1863
7135	Vickery. Wm		A	1	S. S...	Aug.	2N	1864
13090	Vincent, James		K	8	Cav.	Feb...	22	1865
9906	Viled. Nelson		D	22	Inf...	Sept...	2N	1864
1407	Vogle. Jacob		G	27	"	May...	29	1864
4960	Walker. Geo		G	22	"	Aug...	5	1864
1701	Walker. Henry		C	22	"	June..	6	1864
3301	Wunderly. Adam		F	5	Cav.	July...	14	1864
4410	Warne, Hurvey		B	4	Inf...	"	31	1864
11090	Warner. James B		K	5	Cav...	Oct...	1N	1864
11037	Washburn. Sidney		E	1	S. S...	Aug...	9	1864
7302	Way. Thos. H		C	7	Cav...	"	31	1864
4721	Weidman. Harrison		H	1	S. S...	"	4	1864
7902	Wells. Francis		I	7	Inf...	Sept...	3	1864
7312	Whalen. Hiram A	Sergeant.	I	6	Cav...	Aug...	26	1864
9644	Wheeler. Elisha		B	24	Inf...	Sept...	27	1863
733	Whipple. Geo G		A	4	"	Apr...	25	1861
340	Whitaker. Joseph F		B	7	Cav...	"	2	1864
12723	White. Christ		F	5	"	Mar...	3	1865
2499	Whitlock, Marcus L		H	2	Inf...	July...	1	1864
12794	Whittmore. C		M	8	Cav	Mar...	1N	1865
9525	Whitworth. Wm. G		A	6	"	Sept...	22	1864
9076	Wilder. Hamilton S		K	23	Inf...	"	11	1864
6741	Wiley. Edward T	Corporal.	E	1	S. S...	Aug...	21	1864
3190	Willetts. Stafford L	Sergeant	K	22	Inf...	July...	20	1864
3651	Williams. Nelson (or Melton)		A	1	Cav...	Aug...	8	1864
5706	Williams. Theo		C	2	"	"	15	1864
741	Wilson. Byron		D	5	"	Apr...	26	1864
957	Wilson. James		K	22	Inf...	May...	11	1864
2102	Wilson. Wm. W		I	11	"	June..	17	1864
12907	Windlass. Silas		K	8	Cav...	Dec...	1N	1864
9022	Wing. Albert		G	17	Inf...	Sept...	17	1864
4961	Wingarden. Abraham S		K	1	Cav...	Aug...	7	1864
1920	Wolfe. Frank'n		E	13	Inf...	June..	14	1864
3137	Wolverton. Chas. F		B	6	"	July...	17	1864
6596	Wolverton. John S	Sergeant.	A	5	Cav...	Aug...	27	1864
8331	Wood, Ammon O	"	M	6	"	Dec...	20	1864
3992	Woodruff. Henry		C	1	"	July...	28	1864
11242	Woous. Fred'k.		E	24	Inf...	Oct...	21	1864
11323	Wolfinger. H		H	12	"	"	24	1864
1099	Woo'sle. Robert M		E	22	Inf...	May...	4	1863
749	Wright. Wm. A		K	7	Cav...	Apr...	26	1864
3969	Wright. Wm. H		K	5	"	July...	13	1861

MICHIGAN SOLDIERS IN ANDERSONVILLE NATIONAL CEMETERY.—*Cont.*

No. of grave	Name.	Rank.	Company.	Regiment.	Arm of service.	Date of death. Month.	Day.	Year.
2910	Yacht, E	Sergeant	E	22	Inf	July	5	1861
9536	Yorke, C		K	5		Sept	22	1863
2626	Zett, John		D	22	Inf	June	2	1864

The following named were removed to Andersonville National Cemetery from sundry localities in Georgia

13516	Barrett, Warren (Removed from Milledgeville)		D	13	Inf	Nov	22	1864
13506	Bowman, Edwin M. (Removed from Milledgeville)		G	1	Eng	"	24	1861
13678	Cashmore, C. M. (Removed from Louisville)		H	13	Inf	"	28	1864
13215	Caselman, Wm. T. (Removed from Macon)		M	8	Cav	Sept	30	1864
1313	Duning, E. (Removed from Macon)		K	12	Inf			
13071	Eisden, M. T. (Removed from ——)		K	12		July	13	1862
13697	Hines, John (Killed in conflict with 1st Wis. Cav. at capture of Jeff Davis: first buried at Abbeyville. Removed here)		E	4	Cav	May	10	1865
13248	Huff, Lyman P. (Removed from Macon, Shiloh Prisoner)		B	1	L. A.	"	15	1862
13533	Ives, Homer Levi (Removed from Sunshire)		G	8	Cav	July	31	1864
13079	Mills, James (Removed from Macon)		I	12	Inf	July	10	1862
13209	McDonald, Donald (Removed from Macon)		E	2	Cav	July	28	1865
13962	Millspaugh, Thos. A. (Removed from Milledgeville)		F	13	Inf			
13696	Rupert, John (Killed in conflict with 1st Wis. Cav. at capture of Jeff Davis: first buried at Abbeyville. Removed here)		C	4	Cav	May	10	1865
13240	Ruperts, S. (Removed from Macon)		F	8	Inf	Feb	25	1865
12386	Stillwell, J. (Removed from Macon)		E	12	Inf	Aug	15	1862
13077	With, S. (Removed from Macon)			12	Inf			
13304	Worden, Alonzo (Removed from Macon)		K	2	Cav	June	30	1865

CONCLUSION.

As will be seen elsewhere in this report, the Andersonville Monument Commission received $500 to defray the expenses of the commission. In order to enable the commission to publish this report, they used economy along the line, and after paying all obligations they had a balance on hand of $163.02, which the Attorney General decided could not be used to publish a report. So we turned it back in to the State Treasurer.

Believing the report to be valuable to the State, I drafted a joint resolution asking for an appropriation to publish 500 books, at a cost of $205. The Committee on Military Affairs in the house sent for me; they stated that the book was very valuable and suggested that the resolution should call for printing 1,000 instead of 500, at a cost of $335. The resolution passed both the House and Senate without a dissenting vote, and was signed by the Governor. As a portion of the report, you will find the joint resolution printed in full, showing that the commission had come into possession of valuable information in regard to the 735 Michigan soldiers who died in Andersonville; also in what manner the books are to be distributed.

GEO. W. STONE,

Secretary.

MICHIGAN
DEPARTMENT OF STATE
LANSING

I, Albert Dunham, Deputy Secretary of State of the State of Michigan and custodian of the Great Seal of the State, hereby certify, that the attached sheets of paper contain a correct transcript of House Enrolled Act No. 96, Approved March 30, 1905, the original of which is on file in this office.

In witness whereof, I have hereto affixed my signature and the Great Seal of the State, at Lansing, this 17th day of April in the year of our Lord, 1905.

[SEAL]   Albert Dunham,
                    Deputy Secretary of State.

HOUSE ENROLLED ACT NO. 96.
(Joint Resolution No. 202.)

Joint resolution authorizing the Michigan Andersonville Monument Commission to compile, print, illustrate and bind one thousand copies of their report.

Whereas, The Michigan Andersonville Monument Commission was appointed to carry out the provisions of act number forty-three of the public acts of the State of Michigan for the year nineteen hundred three; and

Whereas, The commission have come into possession of the names, company, regiment, date of death and number of the graves of seven hundred thirty-five Michigan soldiers who died and were buried at Andersonville, which list has never been compiled and printed in Michigan, and which the commission propose now to make a part of their report;

Resolved by the Senate and House of Representatives of the State of Michigan, That the Michigan Andersonville Monment Commission be and are hereby authorized to compile, print, illustrate and bind one thousand copies of their report, forty copies to be furnished to the commission, one copy each to Department Headquarters Grand Army of the Republic and Adjutant General's office of the State of Michigan, one copy to each person who attended the unveiling of the monument at Andersonville, the balance to be placed in the hands of the Adjutant General of the State of Michigan to be distributed as follows: One copy to the widow of any soldier so buried at Andersonville, if she be living; or if she be dead, then to his father, if he be living; if he be dead, then to the mother of any such person, if living; or if she be dead, then to his eldest child, if living, and if not, then to the nearest living relative.

Further Resolved, That the Board of State Auditors are hereby authorized and empowered to pay, out of any moneys not otherwise appropriated, all bills pertaining to publishing said report (when countersigned by George W. Stone, secretary of the commission). The amount appropriated and expended shall not exceed three hundred thirty-five dollars.

This joint resolution is ordered to take immediate effect.

SHERIDAN F. MASTER,
Speaker of the House.

ALEXANDER MAITLAND,
President of the Senate.

Approved March 30, 1905.
FRED M. WARNER,
Governor.